Sai...

Deep

Lord of Light

Sandeep Patel

The Holy Bible (NIV)

[Mark 10:35-45]

The Request of James and John

Then James and John, the sons of Zebedee, came to him. "Teacher," they said, "we want you to do for us whatever we ask."

"What do you want me to do for you?" he asked.

They replied, "Let one of us sit at your right and the other at your left in your glory."

"You don't know what you are asking," Jesus said. *"Can you drink the cup I drink or be baptized with the baptism I am baptized with?"*

"We can," they answered.

Jesus said to them, *"You will drink the cup I drink and be baptized with the baptism I am baptized with, but to sit at my right or left is not for me to grant. These places belong to those for whom they have been prepared."*

When the ten heard about this, they became indignant with James and John.

Jesus called them together and said, *"You know that those who are regarded as rulers of the Gentiles lord it over them, and their high officials exercise authority over them. Not so with you. Instead, whoever wants to become great among you must be your servant, and whoever wants to be first must be slave of all. For even the Son of Man did not come to be served, but to serve, and to give his life as a ransom for many."*

Contents

Dedicated to Trey and our Father

Prelude

A man walks to a patio deck of a grand house with glazed windows:

Knock, Knock!

Who's there?

Samuel!

Samuel who?

Samuel, Samuel of course. Can you see me as black?

Man I missed you, come in.

Before A.D.

One

Survived through idiocracy, through gullibility and for what? Not to know how the difference I could have made played out? However this was only taught to me now, how could I be oblivious to sin? Even the shooter knows why he is firing, but why was I promised to feel nothing when I let everything go? Late books and greasy fries along with reassurance from the right made everything unspeakable. Never mind as hopefully the Day of the Lord will help a dog kneel or fall into the crack that he came from.

If the dog had not witnessed what I went through then there would be no problem but to silently sit and observe the flowers growing around him. I flowered him with love and appreciation with whatever he said even as he didn't say much, and based on the fact that he was blessed much greater than us. He was my confidence patch, Romeo. A simple stranger who I mistakably spoke with and only after ten years I realized that the reason why Romeo didn't say much was because all he had to speak of was lies like my mother.

Irony of the matter was that I, Shankar, met Romeo through a night of religious reformation at the local community centre in Leicestershire, England. A cold night in October and the only warm place to stand happened to be by a radiator that was already occupied at the Charotar Patidar Samaj.

Samaj's (communities) like so many in Leicestershire and around the world were filled with music and dancing of a native ritual through nine days out the year for *Nourta*. (A festival celebrating the Lordess Mother of Hindu's through a mythological passage in *Sanskrit*). However now the celebrations were more like a place to pass time, only a few people considered the spirit of a Lord and actually came to celebrate that, socializing was the main aim of this event. I attended for God, this being consciously or not, I always felt that I should fill these days of the year to show gratitude to my mother's faith.

At fifteen I stood by Romeo towering him easily by a foot and him shadowing me by six years. The first thing I asked him that cold night was which one of the hundreds of girls attending *Nourta* did he have his eye on? The surprising thing was that he had his eye on the same girl that I thought to be most attractive and from then on we were best of friends.

Neither of us tried to speak to this anonymous girl. All I heard from him was that she was older than I and hence not to pounce at that opportunity. Throughout the time I knew Romeo he never took that chance; fair enough, no courage, no humiliation and no loss right?

In spite of this, did he feel pride when I lost after taking a dose of spinach? I never heard sorrow from him. I spent most my time with him complaining in hereditary language how everything was awful and not once I heard from him, 'don't be stupid!' His friend, Tamal, who was his confidence tried to teach me one night, but I placed race before wisdom and disregarded what he said. Later I ended disregarding Tamal, Romeo's childhood friend, Romeo said nothing.

Life has a way of drifting by and slowly so did Tamal, for marriage and children he worked around the clock. I began to grow a beard and we drifted further still. He came to visit me when least expected and now I realize this he was doing for me as then I had plenty of pride to believe I needed him. Through Romeo Hindu's became silently obscure and Allah's truth became dismissed. (*Kudha* forgive me and forgive my elders and give us sight to read Scripture. Amen).

I began neglecting my family and spending more time with Romeo and Tamal. They were older and hence cool and Tamal had his own car, and Romeo apart of the same caste of community, like two Methodists and a Baptist, one for thought and one for love, I felt invincible amongst my own peers.

This I strongly needed at that time of my life as I was a victim of school bullying, "pea-head, pea-head," people cried since some crazy physicist in the sixth grade made that up. I was not raised to stand up for myself so I remained silent with no insult of any form of swear or lyric to shut that from spreading. Pea-head spread extremely fast and before I realized girls called me this to ease their moments of discharge and I still said nothing. Carry on with work and I'll be out of The City of Leicester School, in no time.

This school was famous for well-known celebrities like England soccer stars Gary Lineker in 1984, and Emile Heskey in 1999, and growth of an explosive irregularity in 1996. Well by the time O-levels were done I was drinking but most unfortunately was smoking too. There was no point living at home as home was a place I tried to be away from.

The early days of meeting Romeo and Tamal were harmless; I was still in diapers at sixteen years and followed them around Leicester town, to the slot arcades, and through the mall to the billiard house. We spent most of our time mastering the art of playing eight ball stars and stripes. Conversations were around where the balls were placed and when my next exams were.

Tamal was not fortunate enough to get to university as he was needed at home. Romeo had been to some university in England where he had graduated with some certificate in computing, and the only story that I remember him speaking of was when he got drunk over cocktails and passed out in the toilets of some club. Since then he had stuck to drinking Budweiser. I drank cider even though I wasn't much of a fan for apples, but this drink quenched my thirst and remained filled throughout our hour of passing time and speaking about which girl I thought was hot. At that time hot was classified as who dressed the least, nothing really to do with name or personality as the personality of the girl was just as the crazy physicist's. Nothing really ever mattered in my pea-brain those days besides who would hold the win on that day, Romeo or Tamal? With my money running on Tamal, Romeo upped his stake.

In the ninth grade my confidence rose. I attended afternoon smoke sessions with Huliyo as that comforted my thought process on why Sarah had broken my heart. Huliyo did not forcefully ask me to smoke, but I was stupid and had no other sense of direction or purpose besides fulfilling my grades and trying to be liked by the opposite sex.

Throughout that summer before the change of school venue and the growth of extreme late puberty I had visited my cousin in India, and all his friends, of which all of them smoked. Then back to England with a carton of Benson and Hedges in my pocket ready to begin college away from peas and any other type of vegetable.

I attended Wyggeston & Queen Elizabeth I College, set beside Leicester University; famous for discovering genetic fingerprinting in 1985 by Sir Alec Jeffreys. The campus was beautiful and was attended by an average of all student bodies around Leicestershire. My major was in science and math, and I attended college on a regular basis. No insults, no embarrassments, just plain old living, learning and socializing with most if not all the college. This period of two years to earn A-levels were a highlight of my life. There was life in the air and each day was a blessing of which I thought none the wiser. I finished college with flying colours but nothing on my future agenda besides a hint by a close friend Amos to build a future in dental medicine.

I was confused on which degree to sort. Top marks from year one at college, along with top friends, I had the world at my finger tips and a beat to a drum, but all I knew of was what my elders knew and that was to be a doctor. And not a doctor of psychology or education, but of whom was only heard from ancient India.

Sitting with Amos at lunch I decided to follow his path upon becoming a dentist. Nine to five works, and pay is well, and this would keep the elders grateful. So I applied to universities around England, especially in London, a city far from home and full of opportunity to discover my new born gift, smoking and socializing.

In the meantime I had built a tolerance for alcohol. Studying had not been difficult for me so that left plenty of time with Tamal and Romeo. Tamal introduced me to late night clubbing at seventeen; I easily walked past doormen working for nightclubs aged twenty-one and over. This was not a state in the States, this was Leicester, a town filled with mixed ethnicity and drinking was legal at eighteen. That night Tamal managed "to-score." What a brilliant way to pass time away from books, un-delightful tyranny, and arguments from home, drinking, smoking, dancing and making meaningless conversations with strangers after lights went out. And I managed to make this a routine.

The summer vacation after graduating from Q.E. and before attending university was spent at my cousin's wedding in New Jersey, USA. Romeo accompanied my family and I to America as my mother loved Romeo, and I thought that this would be a great idea, such a great idea that I wished Tamal to come with us too. He had agreed but not knowing full well of his family situation and hence declined. My father hated this financially or just anciently racist and I began to hate Tamal too. Disappointed for myself rather than for him our ties became loose. Romeo said nothing; he remained a silent partner on my side and whatever on Tamal's, overall he enjoyed the vacation.

Back from holiday and now attending the world's most prestigious medical university, King's College London, class of '98, a fantastic new beginning for students from all around and an interesting one for the university. King's College had joined with Guy's Hospital London to bring a new perspective to their teaching; none of this mattered to me at the time. I cared for myself, an insecure individual that hid behind cigarettes whilst opportunity to try and thrive for others began to quietly chip away.

From week one I was nostalgic and not that of home but from Tamal and Romeo. From the first weekend I returned home from London, (this was not a bright idea, but who knew the repercussions of that idea would turn a ripple into a tide? Nevertheless I had no good guidance and all I felt with strength was that received from being with the lads). That weekend I met Lara, in a club, she was wearing a short silver dress and holding a bottle of Budweiser, dancing with her gorgeous hips which moved her hair and her smile that could only be expressed as graceful as a tear. From that night on for a year and a half there were regular fortnightly trips back by rail from London to Leicester back to London. Romeo and Tamal helped arrange Lara and I to meet and to party like there was no tomorrow.

"Your stature is like that of the palm, and your breasts like clusters of fruit. I said, "I will climb the palm tree; I will take hold of its fruit." May your breasts be like the clusters of the vine, the fragrance of your breath like apples, and your mouth like the best wine."

[Song of Songs. 7:7-9]

From the time I failed with Lara, Tamal was more distant than Romeo, probably on the fact that Tamal now was married with children. Romeo was still Romeo and nothing deceived my opinion of him. Throughout my cruel break out with Lara and my twenty-first birthday drug fest and many other alcohol/cannabis encounters there was no control to my behaviour, and no purpose for my actions, with and without Romeo. Yes I felt sorry for him, I had no idea why, probably the anticipation that he may begin to speak freely or have the ability to get married.

Six years now had past and I realized that this stranger was no longer to be spoken with. He was not a great friend or a good friend, matter of fact he was no friend, but I was now obsessed with green leaf that decisions and emotions became erased at every chance I had away from work. I had spoken to Romeo during the last days of my stay in England that I felt cheated by his friendship. Nothing of that made any sense as why should that? I was on drugs multiplied by nth factor and he was sober. I can't remember him ever smoking to the amount I or the others did, but what I can remember about the others is that they spoke freely. Something I expected Romeo, my first friend, whom I considered a brother to do instead of quietly holding open the door to hell and letting anyone holding my hand in. I had no confidence and all I had I sucked out into a spell with the only ones who listened, my friends.

The last memory I have of Romeo was early summer of 2006. An evening by a table, with drinks and laughter, smoke and Butch with a large Rottweiler leashed on an one inch steel chain, anything but Butch's idea. They walked over and sat with us on this warm evening at an outdoor bar beside a canal, and we watched the birds fly and the drinks refill. Then the sunset and I asked the Lord to please let me forget my last ten years.

Two

About my mother, she speaks when she says she'll listen. But probably like some she spoke more and comprehended less. I hated speaking to my mother; she would begin to speak loud, and frustrate herself and then turn my words as insults. This she would use against me as swears when she felt the need for attention or emphasize that she was wrong for raising the devil's spawn. This became a nightmare; I couldn't stand being around this woman. This wasn't an attention deficit disorder the pagan acted selfishly.

First I began to fault myself then I began to fault others, later I understood that the only reason I would want my mother alive was for my sister, who without the Lord in my life would have become just as her. I reserved myself from her, nothing about my life and keeping her questions answered short. The potentiality of speaking about school life, interests, quarries and friends would all become contraindicated. And whoever earned the most in the entire world would be praised and hence I became obsolete. The possibility to love her disappeared, she loved me and she spoke highly to others about me, however she knew nothing about me. And as for the Lord I reached the ability to forgive her continuously. Love God.

"In the beginning God created the heavens and the earth. Now the earth was formless and empty, darkness was over the surface of the deep, and the Spirit of God was hovering over the waters."

[Genesis 1:1-2]

Whilst I was at university my mum's family throughout London and Outer London surrounded me but I chose to live alone. Freshman year was at Denmark Hill, an area of London I never had imagined, and chose King's College Hall as the broacher had a Sikh dude sitting on a deck staring on a cloudy day. I had visited Denmark Hill countless of times as one of my mother's brothers happened to live not even one bus journey away. And the only real time I had personally visited them was when I was living in Norbury in my first final takings of my dental exams which was in 2004, six years after I had moved to London. I kept myself isolated from the rest of the family members as I had a nasty habit of smoking and drinking, things throughout six years got from bad, to worse, to unimaginable. Norbury was my final chance to settle my family's dreams.

The problem had come from a long time before hand. The trust in the relations of my mother for my father's side of the family was lost. All I heard from kinder hood was complaints about how any member of my father's immediate family was a disgrace to her. I had brushed most remarks from her and carried on at eighteen to study in the streets of London.

Now I'm in London from listening from the teachings of my parents and my parents alone. Everything relied on satisfying them in every possible way as especially my mother couldn't tell the difference from a joke and the truth when coming from my lips. Think how these times would hold conversations that were never made. Trust is a valuable identity, some people rely on it and some people don't realise that's what was lost that caused them to go down dark roads. I believe that if there's nothing accountable to trust then trust in humour.

Consider me to have written the rest of the words in drunken state over an all powerful Lord. Call Him what you what, I call Him, Shree Krishna, and the way to reach the Almighty Lord is to know about the teachings of His one and only son, Jesus Christ. I understand my mistakes and those caused on a crying child because there's a law of life governed by Christianity, that each Christian can be considered more than Jesus but to Christ, the Light. I believe through all that you read in my testimony that my wrong doings was simply because I had no one to believe from.

Well whilst I was in my wilderness trying to find my path in my community, I didn't do well with people. Out drinking, and smoking and doing everything but keeping a high standard for anyone to follow.

My time in London was spent with an occasionally cigarette to and from the train station, and to and from clinics at Guy's Hospital. For seven years, not five that I would have imagined by a good performing student. Instead I spent time with friends who enjoyed smoking marijuana and friends who enjoyed daily walks around the city.

I never thought there was something that confident from me. Acting like a professional and talking with those that act like professionals disappeared from my life. The professionals in my life were my dad's brothers, their wives and soon to be in ten years their children. They had each other. I was an average of eight years apart of age compared to my immediate cousins, my immediate family. With this gap I never thought to stay in more contact with my dad's brothers and from what my mum says they found it difficult to communicate with me.

All good people left my life early and they went far. My cousins moved to the U.S. and a good friend to Vancouver. This friend and his just married wife were involved in a car accident that almost left her paralyzed. I happened to stop smoking all together hoping somehow spiritually that she would recover if I stopped blowing fumes out of my own lungs. She recovered with screws in her spine and she was able to walk and laugh. My friend kept his spirit up, but then again he always had a good family to lend an ear.

Unfortunately I began smoking after all my exams were done and my result was published as a fail. Instead of staying clean I lit another smoke and called my family to share the news on Diwali. My family had moved to America, South Carolina, three months before I was to sit my final exams in dentistry for the BDS. That was no problem if they had suggested that there was no need me to push where I was and to gain my rewards from England. My life was in England and a choice of option should have been given to me, I was scared, everything was not as easy when you are doing it alone that I failed. I flew to S.C. where I spent over two months amusing the family and their new friends that nothing was wrong and that the next time will be promisingly good. Not only this but I was not issued a Green Card for permanent residency in the U.S. as I was over 21 but 15 other members of my family were. And for business this move had happened.

That was my second trip to S.C. where the first was only two months prior to celebrate my sister's sixteenth birthday. This time to the South I had become introduced to Jesus a little stronger through a band Remy Zero, and reading T.H. White's; The Once and Future King; on the flight. I willingly walked into a church in S.C. as they were scattered all over the place and I knew of no mandir. I needed a place to think quietly, a moment to find answers in His presence. At the time I knew nothing of repentance and heard of Lord Jesus Christ as a forgiveness deliverer, so I fleeced Him to save me from my sins and not let my name die in vain.

My mother had another brother and two sisters who lived in London, the rest of her siblings were either in India or America. I happened to live for six months with one of her sisters in Wembley. This was after I had failed the third attempt of my final exam and had come back from another stay from the South. When I arrived back to England this time around I was lost, there was nothing for me to do for six months which I spent smoking marijuana and weight lifting, going to feast lunches alone and spending hours at a Moroccan bar getting baked on more skunk.

I travelled to central London from Wembley almost every day, which was an hour journey all because I just wanted a place to smoke. I had no idea what I was doing and stayed silent to hear Jesus lead the way. I had come back from S.C. for the fourth time and situations in my life had become worse still. Nevertheless I wasn't going to lose my new faith in a Lord Saviour, the possibility of hope, and all that the London families lived by, and that was *Jai Shree Krishna* and *Namaste*.

Since worshipping in English I felt strength in my judgment; that everything was lost and there was nothing I could do about that and the only person to rely upon was Christ as I knew of no one else.

After failing the course as a whole, I needed to get my life working. I knew nothing about life, no house buying, no car purchasing, but I had a family in Wembley to live with and they gave a lot of faith. I didn't realize even after I failed my attitude was that of my parents or what they had made me. Walking a path of righteous has showed me that this is not a chore but a desire.

Whilst I lived in Wembley after I failed all, I lived with my listening mother's immediate relatives there I was allowed to speak of whatever I wished. I looked for a job. The job involved running from shop to shop selling a "better" telecom service. I did this until I was laid off as I could not meet their requirements; however I managed to set a few new customers for them and spending days on end doing so I did not get paid. I found another job with health care sales at local public spots in London such as Victoria Station and Liverpool Street Station. Here I did better but not well enough to be held on to work longer. I was laid off that job too. I was paid fairly there for the contracts I had gathered.

The rest of Wembley life was aimed to sanely pass time until returning back to America in summer 2006. There was nothing going for me anymore in London, I couldn't enter back into university as my attempts were final and my appeal fell negative. And I somehow chose the time to smoke and hide the truth from my family for the two weeks of which Guy's Hospital had given me to appeal in winter 2005. I did not appeal as I had enough of life, and if the presence of the Holy Spirit had not approached me the way He did I would not have even seen 2006. For me dying was easier than crying.

The Wembley home was filled with babies and laughter. My mother's sister, her husband, his sister, her son married and blessed with two precious girls, one being a year old, and the other about four and my cousin about thirty four stayed in this house. Their home was actually two houses neighbouring each other with the gardens facing the Bakerloo Line running on the northwest rails of Greater London. There was an average of six trains an hour that whizzed past the kitchen windows; the trains flew by as fast as my time there.

Wembley also gave me time to sit and slow down. I hadn't slowed on the smoking but I did gain the ability to concentrate on what mattered. And for this I thank my *masa* (mum's sister's husband). A man who knew how to cook, never smoked and only drank socially, all other times he would sit at home adjusting his finances and reading the daily paper. An extremely calm individual that on first impressions could be mistaken for a devil himself.

I give this man my life. I sat with him when I was baked, he sat and watched television and I stared at the wall. He peeled veins off tangerines whilst watching television and he helped me slowly build the courage to watch him as he peeled the tangerine veins. By the end of my stay in Wembley on St. John's Road my speech was amended to build periods with confidence in speaking to groups of people. I was however still smoking but now this was to deal with the fact to feel euphoria rather than suicidal. This man helped me open my emotions towards why I hadn't appealed on time and frankly allowed me to speak without being judged or hated.

Mostly for the last six months in England I spent time away from their love filled four walls. I felt comfortable staying isolated due to embarrassment and shame so I remained away from confrontation until I was suited to speak. Most my time was spent in Leicester with Romeo or driving up and down the A1 high as a kite, trying to solve what I should do but instead not solving anything as I was always on the move.

Sometimes I parked into quiet locations to have a smoke and stare out to the horizon and ask God to stop. I really needed an older brother, an older image of someone that fights for what's amazing. Nevertheless at those times I would unnecessarily visit my father's sister's newsagents in King's Cross, to pass the time with their youngest son. He was a great lad, spirits up and very considerate about the person beside him unlike his older brother who cared mostly for himself, nevertheless I did happen to be a bully to both brothers when I was young. I bullied them most the time, one brother realized this was childish stupidity and the other realized this a little later but until then he stayed clear of me. Two separate peas in a pod but both with more sense than I ever had even if they only shared half that sense between them.

If I wasn't in London then I was in Leicester being arrested for drinking excessive amounts and talking to two female police officers. Happened to be that two male officers walked around the corner and arrested me mostly for a male sense of chauvinistic reason for a boast. Being tall made all the reason to be guilty. I hadn't caused any trouble, I was with Romeo and somehow got thrown out a club just after I paid to enter, and then happened to see two female officers whom I was harmlessly talking to, and then along came two male officers who asked me to leave, and amongst slowly staggering away I staggered too slowly and got nicked. Romeo walked home. I spent the night in the cell and went to court the following week; the charge was withdrawn as there was no actual felony involved with the incident besides excessive drinking, and speaking and slow staggering. That day my charge was at zero pounds until I had got back to my car, my car was clamped.

That was my luck when I left England, that was how I left England, confused, drugged, full of alcohol, no common-sense, utter disappointment, no comfort and self-respect, in debt and somehow full of faith in Christ. Probably not out of love but for blame. I needed someone to explain this devastation I had suffered continuously across seven years and somehow I was obligated to hold onto a Jesus to explain my fallings. I'm following a life now believing in the Light, God and my peace.

Three

There's nothing much to say about home. My father moved with his brothers and sisters from Africa after the British-Indian Raj to England, due to grandfather who had happened to have rowed a boat from Africa and passed British customs to settle in Leicester as I was told by my father.

My grandparents' offspring consisted of four sons and three daughters, one married and settling in London, another settling in Leicester and the other past before my birth. My father's three younger brothers' marrying and settling around Leicestershire, all cousins being a few generations younger, except for the oldest daughter's who had two boys, a year older and a year younger than I in London.

My mother was a dramatic woman, through all my witnesses I saw in her worship for *Bhagavan* and through marriage she had never settled into a western world. After marriage she entered this home as the first wife, served her in-laws and began work in textiles for a local factory in Leicester. As early as I can remember our house was filled with my parents, my father's parents, their sons and daughters minus one and my father's uncle. Everyone either worked or went to a university. I remained at home with my grandparents whilst my mother worked. I cannot remember my mother ever speaking highly towards her in-laws, the context of negative expression, and excessive home labour was emphasized into my infant years and then after we had moved into our own home.

She worked and my father worked until they made enough money with my *kakas* (dad's brothers), that they opened several newsagents across Leicestershire. These businesses were managed into my junior years when they were sold and my father with his brothers entered a new market in garment manufacturing. A fashion industry had swept across England and Europe and my families were lucky enough to accumulate some investment for a factory to produce clothing.

My life was distant from my father, through infancy, juniors, to adolescents, into high-school, changing high-schools, through college and into university with an affair, where fate furthered the distance between my father and I.

I was not allowed to ask my father questions or suggest things. This resulted into fear of asking him anything. From youth asking him a question would result into a lie or superficial anger, and his natural tendency to save himself from embarrassment would lead to exasperation towards me for not knowing the answer. My father would physically take me to the police station to scare me as a child if hitting me wasn't enough. My dad had to decide what to scare me with the most, a fist or a leather belt and buckle. I feared him instead of fearing the Lord. The net caring for the boy that cried wolf made me lose my ability to be strong and incisive.

Just like King David from the Holy Bible, the repercussions that my father left from the beginning of my university life would have been well-imagined by a most poorly paid psychologist, however at that time I had no meaning of King David or shrinks.

About a party of breaking brotherhood the time had come when all brothers' had moved and one brother and sister from the village missed out. The brothers had felt awful on believing what I'd believe as they settled in the U.S, after the king had lied guilty on his deathbed to stop village sister.

As for youth I grew up fearing my father and trying not to upset my mother. Once the affairs were revealed in my first year of dental school at halls on a night where my mum found it of importance to drive hundred miles and share this sad news with me. I remember my dad standing at the doorway of my dorm room whilst my ten year old sister sat and listened to my mum exaggerating her truth to me. Through all her negative thoughts to every person (and soon to be me too) she mentioned that my dad's brothers choked her. My dad's brothers had come to my home to calm my mum and dad and comfort my sister, but my mum immediately thought the worse and thought they were taking her away. My dad at the time had abused himself physically out of guilt or that my mother wouldn't stop her tongue to listen to reason. That day I lost my trust. I didn't even know what trust was at that time. Whereas for becoming better I turned worse as now I was free of my dad's fear. Here was when I became lost. There's no God. What is God?

That's all in the past. This was a mistake made by my parents it was not mine to have burden upon. But nevertheless their mistakes and no praises left me lost. My father was a man that when I spoke of intellect I was acting too smart. As simple as speaking English to him when I was young was considered a mistake.

"Fathers, do not exasperate your children; instead, bring them up in the training and instruction of the Lord."

[Ephesians 6:4]

Times were to change more in a matter of three years. Instead of learning to enjoy my university life I was consumed to travel to Leicester weekly. As in three years my family and extended family would leave to move across seas to United States. My family and extended family live as close as South Carolina and North Carolina now. Both my grandparents on my mother's side have passed away and so has my father's father. My father's uncle is still alive at the age of eighty-something with my widowed grandmother. My father's brothers live in North Carolina, U.S.A. and building schools and development in India, where the oldest sister still lives in London, making the youngest sister married with three wonderful children who all live in Leicestershire, the home of the Walkers and Lineker's.

Four

Free-living from freshman year at university from eighteen hit me harder than a ton of bricks. And who better to suffer this than Lara. What she must have thought was always better than what she saw. Everything new, exciting and secure.

Yes time was spent on the phone, and time was spent holding hands and taking walks. Other times were spent going to clubs, and bowling allies, cinemas, to libraries, to pool and snooker halls. I never thought about taking her to coffee shops to sit for hours on end with mocha and speak about my week at university. Instead she was bombarded with noise from my friends and my conversations with them.

I used my friends like Romeo and Tamal to be close to her. If walking from the train station to meet her was not enough then I would have walked to her home to surprise her in the middle of the night. Throw small pebbles at her window and wake her from her sleep or the conversation she was having with her mother.

My weeks at university whilst being with her were spent obsessing about her, constantly calling her and moving away from my newly made friends. This was not her fault by any means. Instead of filling my heart with reasons to love her I filled her heart mostly with my mother's tongue, and that was disappointment either about life or that I was not spending enough time with her.

Bizarrely I told my university friends to shut up when they were trying to look after my own good. I still remember a time when one dear friend approached me whilst I was having an argument with Lara over the phone, and I strongly gestured him to leave and allow me to carry on making noise by the quiet Guy's campus courtyard. I could not control my behaviour as I honestly thought there was nothing wrong with it.

There were times when things were good across the board; times when Lara came to London and all times shared with my first year undergraduate dorm mates. She made friends easily, she was extremely lovable and I hate myself for listening to friends as Richard. I was thick and stupid, where satisfaction did not come from my soul but from the lads where my emotions to love

Lara laid. I behaved as one or both of my parents at times and I began to neglect my life's greatest joy.

There's nothing else to write besides the fact that I argued with her most the time, to try and get attention all the time, even when she was taking a shit. This lovely shit taker gave so much love to me that even after she wanted to split she asked her mother to call me and make up for the new millennium. My year of infamous knocks, call Him what you want as thinking too hard about how to spell millennium will obviously hurt.

The second millennium A.D. was spent in London at the flat of Naomi's new boyfriend, Shaun. Naomi was special, she was what one would describe as a free spirit, a person being the joy of the room and she regarded me as the same. Shaun and Naomi were my classmates and fellow pre-dentists.

"The grace of the Lord Jesus be with God's people. Amen."   [Revelation 22:21]

Shaun however was the only dentist out of us, spiritually as well as academically and whom I considered the coolest dude in our university. This guy on the first week of graduate school bought all his books for the year and started scoring aces across the board. Instead of catching up and looking to catch up with him I was possessed with Lara and finding reasons to live with my home.

Forget you as we were close?! And by the end of the second millennium on the night where the streets of London were filled with noise, and fireworks, singing from Shaun's flat and people building up at the south foot of Tower Bridge we were all free to sin. We walked to Tower Bridge staggering and singing anything full of nonsense that came creatively or absurdly out of Naomi's mouth. That night I remember her shouting and asking me to hold a red flashlight (that I had stolen) high above my head.

"Behold red light of Bethlehem!" she said.

I had no idea what she was taking about, nor did I realize that this sounds like an insult to Christ and that she would begin to lose her best friend the very next day. At the time I thought she's just shouting as she was drunk, but now I am guessing she was filling jealousy over my other arm holding Lara. Rich alcohol was spilt by Naomi and then myself, which was accompanied by another friend's sympathy involuntary production of mixed liquor as Nathan patted my back over one shoulder and regurgitated over the other. Then we ate sewage and fell asleep.

Millennium morning, *aalan wa shallan*, the first concrete face to see was Tamal's. Three guys sleeping on one small room floor and Lara and I on the bed. Tamal sat whilst the other guys left the room to eat and Tamal sat. Somehow what he was trying to let me know I can feel today. The biggest expression of, 'What?!' without moving his lips he stared at me not even once at her early that morning. He looked at me and slowly got up to make some tea. His silence just hit me, he should have spoken, alone I would have heard him, with her I would have heard him, then again *Allah ka shokra* I finally heard.

The time of the millennium was more difficult for me to comprehend now than that was then. I had also made an oath to *Bhagavan* that millennium for the reason He did not make me Jew hence I will no longer eat cow. There have been millions of cows found in oceans and buffalo bones found in lakes but instead of giving alcohol and cigarettes a break I decided to pass off eating beef as a new-year resolution. Then God began to cry and sheltered behind the devil inside of me.

Freedom from my father at home encouraged me to act on impulse rather than thought. All my synapses worked on what shrinks' call id. And my behaviour turned from caring, to smart, to rude, to anger, to superficial and deep torment, to Lara, and then her younger brother, to marijuana, to lose all self-confidence, to gullibility, to appreciation for my brothers, to God, through the closing walls, passed God, to my only brothers, into God, far from family, into myself, on my deathbed with God, above my friends, and further from the reign as kings and from then much further than any form of the truth.

Five

This is the speed to write, the feeling of not knowing when you are writing or the feeling of what you are thinking. This was the feeling for three of my friends Romeo, Vassell and Mike. We all were forced to love to drink; with no reason to actually have a reason to drink we still drank.

Mike drank as his family had no objection towards this, Vassell drank because his rebellions against his father and Romeo drank because his father did and so did the rest of his population of students surrounding him. I began to drink because they did. With Romeo and Tamal I drank cautiously and at the beginning there was no difference to physiological or mental change as there is now.

I hadn't drank for a year before writing this and today I have come home from five shots of liquor, and five bottles of beer and clearly I see what the difference is. I can see past the normality of being sober, that staring at the television whilst typing this very sentence, with no spelling mistakes, no mistakes, all confidence and the only ability to concentrate is for my sister who stares at E.R. on WYFF thinking what the inconsistency was in me now.

Whilst I was drinking occasionally a few years back I did not feel any different. I met with my friends, one, both or all three when I was supposed to meet my family or my girlfriend Lara, but instead I spent the time with them to drink and be a lad.

Romeo was the first choice, he was the oldest and I had spent most my time with him. I would come to Leicester to meet "everyone" but we would end up going out to drink instead. Drinking built confidence and this built strength and there is nothing wrong with strength, which is why I loved Romeo and Tamal. The other two brothers loved drinking on their own accord and being whatever that was I was no one to care.

I admired Romeo as he was a lonesome individual who had survived longer than I had, and he had survived university to accomplish the fact with meeting with me. He was caring, and sensitive and my mother loved him. Probably as he was the same height as her or that he pretended to speak the same language. Either way he built his shallow realization of strength from alcohol. At our age and from the way of his history who was to know that the way we lived was through fertilizer embedded in yeast? And neither of us to know that this way of living was pointless.

Vassell was different; he drank to tolerate the culture derived from home. Whatever they said was not out of love and the only way to tolerate was to find out on our own. We drank when we could and we drank in excess. There was no reason to be shy as when we had a chance to find out where we should stand there was all the time in the world.

In our youth Vassell was isolated in Leicester as for when his father was around, and for the fact that in Leicester he was not allowed to leave home freely. He remained in isolation from communication outside of school hours and he remained isolated from communication over the phone. Vassell drank, smoked and sniffed leisurely when becoming distant from his father. I was surprised when meeting him in Bradford after he had intentionally failed his exams to oppose his father's orders to follow in medicine.

When I met him in Bradford I was already on the path to hell and nothing was going to shock me into a cardiac attack, not even the amount of cannabis he smoked in a joint being nothing less than a field of six feet plants dozen at a time. This was shy of whatever he had to offer, I didn't care, all I felt was Vassell looks up to me, and I have no one to look up to besides the ones I was with.

When he drank as much as a whale alone in the oceans I should have thought for him, instead I joined him and drank for myself. Nothing was to change between us; we were to love each other as we shared more than a homeless man does with his own life than our fathers' did with us. I never told him to slow down on alcohol and when drugs came into play I was in no position to let him know otherwise.

Vassell had a brother; Nicodemus was what we called him. He was a few years younger than us and with me he spent plenty of time with in London. He traveled with me when he needed to and so did his friends. I give plenty of respect to Nicodemus who became a doctor from graduating at Guy's Hospital. I respected Nicodemus as I respected his brother, nothing more and nothing less. I never got to know him as a person.

Smiles and giggles to pass the time away from advice as a professional or was I the professional that he was admiring? Nothing was said due to respect for Vassell and he graduated from two years behind my schedule to graduate, he beats me to the finish line. He was a considerate individual to his own ability; I admired Nicodemus for his interest in learning, his passion to keep following the right path, his concern for his friends and their involvement around university and home.

He learnt from his surroundings and his brothers' misfortunes, he never smoked.

Vassell and Nicodemus were extremely smart and full of wisdom. They knew of sports, science, social societies, economics, business and music. Their interest in music stretched to reading notes, understanding melodies, playing instruments and teaching me a little on the way. My love for the varieties of rock music came much later in my life. Vassell was fortunate enough to start listening to play consonant and dissonant with rhythm from different timbres at an early age. Thus I thank the Lord for him and his brother and ask Him to keep them close to His heartbeat. Amen.

The final brother to have any effect on my life through home and away at university was Mike. Mike was the only child in his family and highly educated with the white society in Leicestershire. His mother loved him obviously and his father loved him dearly too, his family may have loved me dearly as well.

The surprising thing between Mike and I was that his parents had the same name as mine. The first night I spent at Mike's was delivered with post the next morning, this mail was addressed to the same name as my father's, I asked him what his mother's name was and to our surprise they were pretty much the same. And from then we were best of friends.

The Lord should have been respected at this time instead coincidence was played, and autumns changed into summers, which rolled into springs, which revolved into winters. And the appreciation between Mike and I remained with the similarity of the necessity to drink and take drugs than the actuality that we were met through God's Word.

My faith in God, *Allah*, the Lord, *Vishnu* or Father was compromised through Mike. Mike was more atheistic than hopeful and this worked outstandingly for him. Mike knew of only one and that one was his mother. With her knowledge and wisdom he did well, well enough to make a successful career in London. He did exceptionally well considering he managed to do this alongside alcohol and pot. I admire Mike more than I miss him as he did this unwillingly of any faith with no superstitious spirits or love from Christ.

He learnt well from his surroundings but he never advised his surroundings of his teachings. Sometimes I wonder if his confidence came from my faith in God as well as the fact that he wanted to make his mother happy. Either way I am overwhelmed with his success alongside his path that the Lord placed before him, filled with alcohol and narcotics that somehow had no effect on his mental synapses to communicate with his family and friends.

My friendship with Mike was stronger than that of Vassell and Romeo despite that I had known him for less time. I greatly related to Mike as he drank and he lived close with his own car at seventeen, and for the freedom that his family gave him over to that of Vassell's family. Romeo was greatly over the age of Vassell and Mike however lacked all the confidence that they did to speak, and Mike related to this as equal as I. And this helped me relate to Mike closer than that to Romeo.

I relied on Mike to provide reassurance, and Romeo to provide comfort with Vassell to provide strength. I provided nothing to my brothers besides their necessity in me and my reassurance that came from the Lord, willingly or not my existence or what they desired from me was in the control *del Espiratu Santo* or alcohol and drugs.

What they thought of me was never on my mind. With drugs and alcohol running through my bloodstream and without any personal common-sense in the twenty-first century, I asked fewer questions and comprehended with silence when conversations turned from two, to three, to four or five. I stopped listening, especially when football was spoken about. I began to watch football in my early twenties extremely late compared to all my peers. Finally I began to accept that they know more, more in everything. And what was best was if I stopped thinking for my own personal world and coincided with the world I was around. The loss of consciousness I had felt from the beginning of university I felt regret everyday that that was my time to shine and from my life at college there was nothing to stop me.

Vassell knew I was known across Leicestershire probably due to the reason of speech, and height and the only one having a true effect for folk gossip. Mostly Vassell admired that I was carefree to be affected by what people thought. I never intentionally caused trouble in the interest of crime. However some of my actions led me into the night with a smoke in one hand and more on the table asking questions and repenting without ever waking up the next morning. The guys I knew were definitely much smarter than I and with our time together I was not to know that.

"that everyone who believes in him may have eternal life." For God so loved the world that he gave his one and only Son, that whoever believes in him shall not perish but have eternal life. For God did not send his Son into the world to condemn the world, but to save the world through him."
[John 3:15-17]

Whereas for Romeo and Tamal, (Romeo being slightly younger than Tamal), they lived in a rough neighbourhood that deceitfulness gave them knowledge and understanding, like a million others this was for personal gain rather than to be humane.

The times with Romeo were great in some sense as I had a *compadra* that drank. He spoke when he did, however I wasn't much of a person to listen. Maybe if he said something after a "final fight" in terms of anger on my behaviour I may have realized that as a reason to respect Romeo. I enjoyed his company whilst we were on the same page of Scripture written in *Sanskrit* until I spoke about Jesus nine years into our friendship and he used blasphemy instead of interest to reprehend. Things began to get clearer however now there was only time to repent rather than to forget.

Mike and I spent most nights in bars and clubs when we were in Leicester, or in London or in Kent where he had studied. I had good communication skills when we were together or around the other two, however when we were with anyone else a contest brew for Mike and instead of competing I held back. Let him have his glory I have no satisfaction on out witting Mike through his friends. I know he would become frustrated with that, however he may not have. Mike derived talent to speak to strangers at the beginning of his university life where as I paid all attention to Lara and opposing my father.

Mike, Vassell, Romeo and I mostly spent our times together or without one another in Riley's; an American styled pool hall. The mercy of the building held a more authentic type of contest in snooker matches that we mostly checked. Here was mostly a reasonable place to smoke or make a smoke, or drink and/or sometimes as we would say, 'kill time.' Either way I learnt nothing whilst we spent time there. The world turned and I achieved nothing more than a break of eight.

With our last days together I insisted there be no pool hall, with Vassell having plenty of abdominal cramps due to his Crohn's he should have just asked to sit in the car in the middle of nothing and smoke. There was no effect to this man and marijuana for him marijuana helped the pain and passage of stools. When the world began to grow both internally amongst friendship and externally through crime I became stupid and lazy, if there's a difference? And if there were then the worse from the two would most probably be lazy. Christ can most probably teach a stupid person so to sum us up; we were stupid and I was lazy.

Six

When there was no sense in direction there was Jesus in the wilderness, and I in a parallel universe alongside his emotion and that was with no emotion.

What occurred after feeling relief from a schizophrenic disorder was comforting. No voices in my head about hate and I definitely felt no anger. I wasn't upset and that felt great. That was what I'd like to be all the day, should be all the time, why should I have resent, and why should I assort this on others? That obviously would not be fair on whomever I was with and I had no joy in bumming people out. Without feeling remorse I felt healthy mentally. Most of all I felt at peace with my surroundings, along as I had mary-jane by my side nothing else mattered. I knew I wouldn't be rude or project anger to anyone, just like a grounded tree.

The spoils of youth had made me corrupt and now there was no one in my path to let me think otherwise. I lived my life peacefully, no need for anyone as long as my work got done. Then again there was no work, just regret that without marijuana I would not be able to get my work off the floor. The regret for smoking the ganja got the ball rolling slowly and as long as there was a constant supply of sedatives I was o.k.

The year of new prospects and goodwill couldn't have started out any worse. Third year of university and narrowly escaping a sudden flight back from Orlando due to results from a retake exam I should have felt saved. At the time however I had studied hard for two exams, which I failed the first time around, and these two being my first in my life, but I felt confident enough to re-sit them and the next day fly to Orlando with Romeo and his fellow work mates. And I had passed as expected and instead of the vacation falling short we traveled to Miami and had a merry old time.

The blind man polishing teeth whilst looking at them instead of concentrating on the back of the throat deserved no reward. That should have been my final close and I should have packed buddah in for the last time. But somehow I didn't, as the first thing I did before I had unpacked my suitcase at my new apartment at Redman House in London was smoke pot. A bright beautiful day and I rushed my family including baby sister away so I could get settled in. That year all was to change, the Lord had his hand on me as surely the devil was itching to receive me, unless they were pending me for what was still yet to be, *la afham*, I don't know.

Beginning of 2000, the simplest year in dental education that King's had to offer and by far simpler than the year previous, my mind was set on passing time rather than accumulating quality wisdom. Away from Lara and my flesh craved for reassurance, speaking to Mike and how he was doing well whilst still being heavily sedated I had no reason to change myself.

Alcohol and mixed tobacco with cannabis till two months prior to finals should prove satisfactory to move into the fourth year, that would have been enough. So the cycle started. First I tried to make a move on Samantha whilst in this state of euphoria, this made me feel ashamed to see her in class and around university, completely embarrassed of myself and no Jesus to have taught me to say sorry. This led me to sin further and at a much greater depth. A night in October a coach full of students to attend a night out in Brighton in a flash turned my fate from hero to negligent for everyone.

I still can't get why this night occurred, there was no sense in my actions, and the night began with familiar friends and Naomi who was under some sort of depression from Shaun, or from some sort of other situation she needed to get away and be with others.

That night to Brighton I had shared a smoke with the lads on the coach and once into the club we all began to drink. Naomi drank like a fish and with every moment had to be kept an eye on. We were in amongst strangers and she had a way of receiving free drinks and then being louder than usual. This, along with her depression pills she was extremely flirtatious. (What I have learnt now is that girls would like attention and the only attention that comforted her that night was from me). At the time I was clueless, she was a close friend, and I only wanted to be drunk, and high, (and pass time), and by looking around the room there was no one that could compare to Lara.

Half way through the night I smoked another joint with the lads whilst the girls looked over Naomi and by the time we came back into the club people were outside. A fight was brewing between two lads and Naomi thought she could resolve the situation which ended up with her being knocked out cold and falling to the floor. I happened to lift her and place her into the coach.

The ride home was filled with red eyes and mixed emotions with her lying on my lap and I silently trying to arouse her, what was I thinking? She was a friend, she had a boyfriend, who was a good friend, but she did try to have her hand in my pants all night and if I hadn't had resisted then maybe something may have happened between us.

On that ride I thought about arousing her, to wake her and not think about what would happen next. Would she feel disgusted was not what I thought. The way things were going that night I honestly thought she would wake and stick her tongue down my throat. This was all beside the main point. I didn't have feelings for her the way her boyfriend had. And the way the night unveiled I accounted that she had feelings for me greatly over him. Trying to find sense for placing my hand down her blouse past an hour she got up and moved to the back of the coach. (Where I wish I had dropped her before acting stupid that night). I felt scared and followed her to the back seat where the rest of the lads were and pretended to sleep the rest of the way home.

I remember talking to her the next day and denied any truth in what happened, making a phony reason that I was checking to see if she still had a pulse. I can still remember her saying that she would have accepted an apology; all she wanted was the truth, but I was weak in apologies, they didn't make sense to me, the only thing that made sense was to smoke some more and forget that ever happened. I shattered like a grand porcelain statue hit by lightning to dust and from then further still to make sure no one had any reason to remember my existence.

University life crumbled away slowly, embarrassed to see her, embarrassed really to see anyone. Strongly associated with smoking that whatever I thought and whoever I spoke to, and whatever we spoke about ended with one image and one image alone, and that was of me with puff the magic dragon, he'll make everything smooth. Lectures were first off my agenda as I couldn't face seeing her, and only if I had apologized and only if I had stayed off the drugs long enough then I would have been able to apologize. But this was not easily going to be the case, *en seguida que?!*

Later in February 2001 I got my first arrest. Just when I felt that this was the end of the smoke-fest I happened to be used in a stag operation by Metropolitan Police of London. They had their eye on a young potential non-tax labourer and decided to jump on me as well. (He said he found it, that's what he said, found it whilst watching where he going). I was extremely ignorant and during interrogation I shared a few details hoping that this would help my supplier stay away from what I assumed the police already knew. I was released with caution, and for the majority of that year I remained concealed, away from school and away from life, due to fear that this was my entire fault.

That year I failed both my exams and I hadn't stopped smoking. As now being around drug dealers provided me with mental safety. Instead of packing drugs away I became more eased with them; thanks to the police they somehow helped me saturate the comfort of smoking freely. They also helped me define how commercial justice would fail every-time if not working with theodicy. Now I can be thankful for as I am free from fearing the law. Nevertheless the bigger picture was that I still had to pass exams.

Seven

Entering into the new academic year with the rest of my starting year was the year to shape up. God happened to give me a little more confidence as He introduced me to a beautiful Scottish-Indian lass by the name of Jessica. Jessica and I had a fond liking of achievement and education as she loved to learn. She was studying at Guy's Hospital for a B.Sc. in Human Biology and wanted progression into a Medical Certificate once she achieved that.

This gorgeous girl of 5'3" was like a gift that helped me pass both my re-sits with flying colours. I should have held her close to my heart for eternity making amends for my past love; however Jessica clearly did not have the type of love for me as Lara. Jess had a nasty habit of frustrating and accumulating dishonesty. I was to have left her when she happened to spread a lie on the first week of our relationship; however I didn't want to be that guy again and let that pass.

For a year we really enjoyed each other's company. She helped me gain access into the fourth year of dentistry and I helped her to gloat about her new boyfriend to her friends. We went dining, and for walks around London, and to movies and theatres. I met her father who I can like because he was humble and successful, and I admired him for his courage in being an Indian man making ends meet in Scotland. I was overwhelmed to hear that a family outside Leicester away from one's own culture had done so well that I admired Jessica for being the same.

Throughout our relationship one thing remained on my mind, the incident with the police and the attitude of my drug-dealer. I had not told Jessica about this, she was far too lovely to curse with these dealings I had six months prior to meeting her, instead I carried on smoking. She had never touched a cigarette let alone any form of narcotics and she did not complain on me doing so.

I tried numerous times to come off marijuana, this drug wasn't fair on either of us and I was unaware that the drop would make me feel anger. A wish told to last a few days away from the drug to let the downsides pass. However I blamed myself again by feeling remorse and comforted my emotion the next day by lighting another joint.

If I wasn't smoking in her presence I would be smoking with my cousin Sandra's flat-mate Melissa, and if I wasn't smoking around them then I was smoking alone, away from embarrassment of Naomi, and peers and out-aloud at Redman House fearing a response from God. Why I remained isolated when the world was granted at my fingertips I can only blame on smoking. A regret to stay smoking and scared to live a normal life upon fear that this too will be taken away by an attack on myself or with the ones I love.

Reassurance came slightly from Ronald, my flatmate, the only one that knew about what had happened in February 2001; but I stayed far from him too. Clearly I was still afraid and not really recovering and the closer Jessica and I got the further I wanted us to become.

Summer of 2002, Romeo, Mike and I went to India. I had failed my one exam of the forth year Dental Public Health and was to have a new sitting in November 2002. Regardless of that I aimed to leave cannabis once and for all in the vacation to India. Us lads had a whale of a time but gathering away from drugs I substituted this with alcohol. We partied till late in India. Mike and Romeo were as fond as drinking as the whale we were spending time with than feeling regret upon nothing really changing in our lives. I attended the weight-room till breakfast, slept a little till lunch, and after felt numb around silences of Romeo and Mike that the only thing to liven a holiday back to its feet would be more alcohol.

Two weeks passed and I wished we had made more of the holiday. We still enjoyed this vacation, nevertheless I was in India but around Mike this seemed more like the west, and I encouraged this further as between Romeo and Mike, Mike spoke. Somehow I wished Romeo spoke, his culture matched mine vastly more than that of Mike and I, but as Mike communicated Romeo didn't. Maybe I should have spoken for Romeo. Maybe I should have announced that we would not drink and instead visit the mandirs, churches, malls, and markets that Mumbai had to offer. Unfortunately these neurotransmitters had been inhibited for some time now and the vacation was happily spent spending.

Back from our vacation and still as spoilt as a rich fat kid in a candy store. Jessica was in Scotland and my potential fifth year classes had commenced, and so had my smoking habits. I had smoked so much in my time to this point that I'm surprised that I could still spell my name. I never debated to use a bong or a pipe for a clean crisp smoke. This would have proved healthier than mixing cigarette tobacco with skunk. But in my naïve mind smoking a small amount of raw weed in a pot would be worse than wrapping tobacco and massive amounts of bud in rolling paper. Plus the rolling paper would last as I had nobody and nothing else to pass time with. Refilling the pot with clean weed was neither an option or a decision as everyone I knew who smoked, smoked as I did and I never kept a bowl as that would have been too much to hide.

What I thought clearly did not make sense as what I thought was nothing but how to keep my soul in my flesh. Who I was had disappeared and now I was filled with remorseful memories of how things could have been better, and so the only method of remaining intact for my family too became artificially.

As November 2002 approached I was feeling tense, battling between this form of living and concerns for Jessica as she came back from Scotland that I began to rebel against myself. To my surprise she had begun to play events to frustrate me further, dropping old boyfriend names, accidentally sending text messages that were not meant for me, and lying about where she'd be at lunch and who she would be with.

At this point in my life I was not the jealous boyfriend and I was quite far from puff the magic dragon, however I appreciated honesty, whereas I think she would have appreciated a slightly jealous boyfriend and arguments arose. I felt like this was working, she was beginning to hate me and for me that was good. I was still with concern for her wellbeing and with her acting aloof a possibility of burning the bridge became clearer.

That October I accidentally met the drug-dealer and now after a year and a half felt more terrified for Jessica rather than myself. I happened to give him money so he'd leave me alone. I owed him nothing, I hadn't mentioned his name to the police and I hadn't been the one the police were following, the attention the dealer brought on himself was by himself however I was to suffer.

From then to November of my re-sit exam I completely fried any relationship with Jessica. That November I failed the exam and was sent back a year to try again for spring 2003. For a week I disappeared to Bradford to visit Vassell, a city known more for drugs and bad weather than for religion and righteousness.

Christmas of 2002 passed with my family and with my attractive cousin Sandra allowing me to occupy her flat in London with Romeo, Mike and two of my college class friends, Jennifer and Mona. Christmas was filled with laughter, drugs and alcohol, and without submission of what had really happened. I had failed so much that I was surprised that the doctors at university had not advised a strong counsellor. I needed someone anonymous to speak to, no friend or family member and definitely not Romeo. Someone to advise me what I know now, that depression will follow drug rehabilitation and that my faith in God alone can be as strong as Lara's affection.

A Reverend was met before the start of the new term. He seemed as a gentle man, but what did he have to really teach me? Nevertheless instead of asking for help and shutting up, I made up as my life was a problem, and had been for some while. The Reverend said a few things and I was left to carry on the rest of my life.

2003, the class of '98 was about to graduate and I would feel more comfortable getting my butt back into classes and the swing back into my life. No more Naomi to feel confusion about and no more of her lies that may have spread around that year. The time to concentrate and qualify with flying colours. I passed time by greeting and treating patients, along with library sessions to practice taking National American Dental Board Exams, and eating right with occasional visits to the weight-room. Far from anyone I knew at university, and far from Jessica, and further still from the student bar but still close to marijuana.

Now I smoked for another reason, to keep my enemies close. I had no enemies but the thought of the fear of the ex-drug-dealer wanting more money or my head. And hence remained in the circle of narcotics with Mike, Vassell and Romeo and began studying for a way out without concentrating on where I was. I successfully unsatisfied examination requirements again in spring 2003 to be given a final chance with this exam in November 2003. Overall I still had not found the root to my problems and that was to have a healthy relationship with my parents, only then could I have had a stronger relationship with my younger sister and immediate family. I spent time with people that didn't inspire me.

The summer of 2003 was spent in Houston at my cousin's wedding; time away from drugs and alcohol and with the company of loved ones. I managed to act positive and with strength as there's nothing more pleasurable than a neighbouring Indian family wanting to see their close-ones doing worse than them. This gives everyone something to talk about and this would up-set my mother dearly, as her sisters gathering under the same roof to leave marriage arrangement to instead discuss the downfall of my mother's upbringing from start to finish. I would not let this happen and stayed in full spirit to glorify the special occasion for my cousin and to hide the truth from my family.

Time passed and I did too, thanks to an external examiners comfort and encouragement at a pass/fail viva. This viva was a borderline examination criterion as the written paper was not considered as a concrete pass. I was called from dental clinics to attend this oral examination a day after schedule and during this examination the examiners would conclude if I should enter the final year. I remember sitting on a park bench within the Guy's campus before the exam as a nervous wreck. The external examiner approached and sat beside me. He asked me a question and I started blabbering words. He advised me to take a walk for ten minutes and possibly hug a girl. I don't know what happened in that viva. It was like something controlled my conscience and my tongue. The questions were familiar and I answered each question with pose and accuracy. Thanks to him I started with confidence and finished stronger to return back to clinics that afternoon as a final year student.

Eight

An intense moment of my life where everything should have fell into place but considering all possibilities they were bound to face annulment. My life became well. I was living soundly and moderately on part-time marijuana during the evenings, and began to concentrate further on my surroundings and my situations beginning at school. However the problem was not from school but from home. I was scared of my parents' reactions. Their tendency to frustrate themselves deafened me and it hurts me to say this.

My mother announced that my school life was not my fault that the teachers had something against me and she had the same problem when she was young, and this was all because of *naseeb* (fate), that this happens to me, and hence I believed her and by much later I began to hate *naseeb*. The dear woman complained over and over again, some I understood but other times I think she was asking for pity but let's not call this pity as we would insult her further, and she will deliver what she has onto me and that was hate for the world. Deep down inside she resided love. A small drop of love for life surrounded by millions of hate cells covered by a superficial layer of love, and how she reflected to me for all years was that I was to resolve her discomforts, even though one of her discomforts was my father. Caressing her as a person and that special of my mother as advantage I had no thought of nonetheless. I don't know what mattered most to my mum, me or society, that same society that lives depending on income.

I carried on the final year attending a few number of classes and clinics becoming more familiar with my teachers and classmates. Unfortunately no way enough for what was demanded from me. I had missed loads of clinics and especially lectures since '98 that communications with students became artificial, especially from my part as one day I would be in class and the other not. I mostly had done this to keep everyone at arm's length as I believed I was stupid or my presence scared people. All I had to do to reassure myself was to look at my own heart or in the presence of others look at their heart to show them that I cared.

Every other week I returned back to Leicester to find reassurance in my family, however I spent most the weekend out with Romeo or whoever was free. This led to my parents being upset and by the time the weekend was over I was back in London on Sunday evening at Redman House, "high" enough not to remember Leicester, and start late enough on Mondays where at times I missed a whole morning or at times a whole day.

The clinics on Mondays were of orthodontic and pediatric classes which I enjoyed but somehow felt compelled to miss, which then became easier and easier. I began not to care, nor did anyone else, why I didn't care was probably because I always had money in my pocket and regret in my heart that there was nothing fueling the other to succeed. So I needed something else in my life to pass time.

Academic year of 2003-2004 a smooth ride in the final year, do not date, not because this would distract my studies but this would distract my time towards drugs. I needed another release too; I somehow always needed some release of tension that I somehow created for myself. This creation of unbearable necessity for discomfort I found in 2006 came from my father. I couldn't explain why I accumulated enough negatives to make my blood boil in the past until I heard my father once on a quiet journey back from work disrupt peace into chaos. And then I found myself sitting and placing my hands together and bowing my head for nth amount of time by the Lord to provide me with guidance on how to handle that.

However in London there was no Lord, there were gods but why they were important nobody was wise enough to teach me, especially around rattling train tracks, screaming sirens, thundering heels rapidly sounding to one rhythm and unbearable lies from everyone that there was no room for God's truth. Instead I joined another gym, somewhere that was more affordable than the last and soon did my cousin Sandra, and a cycle of weight training, bad Mondays, worse Fridays, and spending glorious brighter and warmer days with the neighbourhood youths by the riverside became a comfortable pass time. The spring of my twenty-forth year into manhood was comfortable enough for me to happily roll a joint on the lawn of the Tate Galleria by the River Thames and smoke this either by myself or with James, a neighbourhood youth.

Nicholas was another neighbourhood youth whom I admired. He was old enough to drink in London but along with smoking he didn't. I think Nicholas admired me due to my confidence in society or interested in evaluating my stupidity. Either way I hope he is well, wise, and wealthy and still can remember the day when I asked for a store bag to shop lift a videogame. Saint Nicholas could not afford the video game and I liked the dude, also I wanted to see if I could blindly change the queen of hearts to the queen of clubs as well as Turkish. Clearly I did but maybe I should have thought on how to change the queens into kings and that of spades, and *que sera sera* orthodontic and pediatric qualifying exams were failed, hence the fifth year was to be repeated.

I happened to start looking for jobs as I had become a bigger burden to my family than before (smoking marijuana eased this concern). I walked along the River Thames, and across The Millennium Bridge, through Embankment, and up to Charing Cross Station asking for job vacancies in every bar and pub along the stretch, to and around Trafalgar Square also. I managed to find a well paying bar job at The Griffin, Bar and Restaurant, Charing Cross.

That time in my university life I can say felt good. The anxious feeling away from the drug arrest was beginning to fall and standing on my own two feet felt well. Late summer Gregg (the bar manager), helped me transfer to Global Café, Bar and Restaurant, in Leicester City Centre. To thank Gregg the plan was to work for the new boss for a month and return back to The Griffin for the new fall. Instead I made some awful excuse and quit the job at Global Café to go to Tunisia with Romeo, his sister Peninsula, her friend Brandy, Nathan, Danny and Arnold. An awful decision to make, this mistake was the worst I made in my life. At the time I occasionally did marijuana however I was experimenting with cocaine and alcohol too. Romeo's friends were clean; my partners were mostly Mike, Vassell and Romeo, along with new associates at university.

"do not plot evil against your neighbour, and do not love to swear falsely. I hate all this," declares the Lord.

[Zechariah 8:17]

Then came the beginning of fall 2004, dropping the job and later dropping Shakira for the chance to move and have a new life in the States. She was beautiful, confidant, sexy and personally the last chance from God for anything good to happen in my life whilst I lived in England. First I didn't grab her when she clearly said she wanted me, I went to Tunisia with Romeo. What was I thinking? (Baby I was wrong not to think you didn't run me any sooner). Leaving a healthy new relationship, dishonouring my employer and for someone who had no regard for my wellbeing. With me in the picture the trip would be cheaper, and I will be able to get a final vacation with Romeo before graduating and moving to the States.

When coming back from Tunisia I dated Shakira for a moment's time only. Now consciousness playing a little on my mind, no future plan with her as twelve months till new life with family and tying all loose ties that were broken at the beginning of my university life fell onto this son of a broken Gujarati family of Leicestershire. So away from Shakira and back onto drugs, couldn't afford to break her heart later, so I decided to force the break up one month into our relationship and one month into the final repeat of the final year. Now two years behind graduation and new flat-mates but with the same old habits.

Here in my life I found pity on a person that was extremely selfish, more selfish than I. Her name was Tanya; she pretty much had everything, a steady job and a comfortable life style in London. The day I met her she was having arguments with a guy that was trying to break up with her, he ended up swearing and this reminded me of a time when I was behaving the same towards Lara. However this guy wasn't doing this for attention, he seriously wanted her gone and I wish I had realized that sooner. Tanya was of no reason to enter into my life now, but I was a sucker for damsels in distress, even though she was neither she was very good at making me believe that she was.

"Do not take your servant for a wicked woman; I ... praying here out of my great anguish and grief." Eli answered, "Go in peace, and may the God of Israel grant you what you have asked ..." She said, "May your servant find favour in your eyes." ... ate something, and her face was no longer downcast."
[Samuel 1:16-18]

She liked to complain about how everything was against her and I liked to get high, so that didn't really matter, and I began to see sites of London that I think were the only good thing about our time together. The suits and skirts of business people rushing into tube stations and in and out of bars between their shifts at the office, a pompous type of imaginary that everything was better there than anywhere else. The truth was that their lives were what I and any homeless man would dream of, a study flow of routine with an occasional cold drink with friends and maybe a hot balti from Brick Lane once a month.

I on the other hand had watched way too many movies. Tanya was a friend with Mike who by this time had achieved what he had seen with his mother. And I am glad that I got to see this too. Mike qualified for a work program at Tanya's company and on a cold raining night during drinks I happened to meet Tanya. Whereas Mike was acquainted with her through business I was through leisure. I felt like I still needed guidance in my life and her being successful could help me achieve what I still had to. She was to provide me with stability during my last era of education. The only person I heard at this time asking me to concentrate was Mike.

Mike and I were 25 when he had moved to London from Canterbury where he had graduated in Computers and Business. His family had helped him acquire a flat just beside the Millennium Dome and I was extremely happy to have him move. Mike liked to smoke as I did, so for more than my free time away from Tanya I spent with Mike. I don't now how the young chap became successful, maybe through what his family had taught him, maybe through his courage or most likely both, I couldn't be more happier. He had climbed whilst taking plenty of narcotics through the teaching program with Tanya, over two other jobs and by the time I left for the States he was comfortably close to a forty grand salary. To Mike and his family I applaud for keeping the little motivation I had left intact during my life at university.

His family was a reflection of mine; his family lived where I hoped mine should have. The hidden contrast between our faiths seemed to have torn me apart. This maintenance of family culture in my western world made me lose everything and smoking to make sense of this for me didn't make any sense at all.

Nevertheless I still did and far after my flat-mates from 2000, Ronald and Gabrielle, had graduated and moved out. 2004 I moved into Ronald's room which was a blessing as the share size was a comfort to be in. Unlike Ronald I pretty much had my door open to the public. The youth of the neighbourhood were allowed to relax there, along with the new flat-mates and his friends, along with Crimson who was a dude that was failing as much as I was and probably smoking the same fair share of cannabis too.

Why did my heart feel pity on others? His friends had neglected him and I should have too or I should have at least encouraged him not to smoke. However these two peas in the same pod were likely to suffer the same outcome. Crimson like everyone else worked around me, and being an addict of fine circles began drinking, smoking and snorting for the majority of that year.

After Ronald and Gabrielle there came Julie and Mohammad. Mohammad began causing rent issues and along with cleaning issues against Julie that they both finally left. Settlement was replaced by Felicia and Patricia, two Italian girls who were the sweetest leaving me to concentrate towards the end of that year. Unfortunately I hadn't satisfied the orthodontic and the pediatric professors and had one more chance in doing so and if to succeed then to pass all requirements along with the final exam in November 2004.

That summer was the last of my insane driven incredulity, and broken inspirations and friendships at Redman House. I made countless mistakes in those four walls, living in the wilderness none of them were consciously made, however I could never feel ease in my life if I didn't have them accounted for. Thank you Jesus.

The landlord of Redman House and I were becoming extremely frustrated with all the people moving in and out that both of us wished for change. I moved to Norbury whilst Romeo discreetly helped my family pack for America. Only when all crates and rigs were filled, photo's taken and printed I was made aware that the move had just happened. As I moved yet into another home my family wished me luck and prayed to *Bhagavan* to help me pass the next time around.

Nine

Opening from my first failure and after arriving back from S.C. I had moved to Weston Street Accommodation. This building was right beside my university and I had six more months to successfully prove myself. The season started in January 2005. Christmas 2004 I asked Jesus in South Carolina to forgive me for my sins and help me succeed this second time.

Now I had fallen almost two years behind and thank Guy's Hospital by signing consent that I had two more attempts at taking the final exam. So I signed that paper like many doctors who signed my attendance sheet so I could pass a fake sheet and pass the Dean's wits. Makes me cry that the doctors couldn't diagnose my behaviour as depression and provide improving diet for management.

All my criteria's were filled, and all that was required for me to do was attend clinics for half weeks and graduate in the next sitting. My act again to begin with was awful; this time I had nobody to blame but myself. My best friends now were Romeo and Vassell who lived in Leicester, and Mike who lived just over Tower Bridge, a stone throw from the sixth floor of Weston Street Accommodation.

Mike enjoyed smoking as much as I did and this new attempt to succeed passed plenty more time for smoking. I had found a quality location where smoking and playing snooker came hand in hand. Actually the first thing I decided was not to spend that much time with Mike but to carry on smoking as now I felt more at ease with what I had to do.

The last part of England became lost as quickly as the rest; and what I had done to my family and myself I cannot possibly begin to imagine. The problem was that I did not want to think anything. I just wished for my time to pass again and that smoking will be the best way to do that. Smoking made me lose the desire to enjoy university.

At Weston Street I remained in my room "watching" movies or looking out the window without a thought about writing this. If I wasn't in my room then I was in Peter's, a freshman who enjoyed smoking too. However I wasn't much at

Weston Street. I was spending most my time with Tanya listening to her day and her obsessions with work. I can see why the Lord had punished me that season. I spent all my time near drugs and Tanya without a care for what was actually good for me or what was Christ like.

When I gained consciousness which was extremely rare I found myself smoking again. Some work was actually done; I attended a few clinics that season and made sure I had everything prepared for my last exam but nothing close to feeling like I should act as a professional. Nor the sense in having any self respect, just resent towards my life and against Buddha.

Living around freshmen and being a student again I neglected placing my hands together, bowing down to the Lord and giving a moment to myself. I wanted things to hurry and finish for once and for all and I would do anything for this time to waste away. If only I hadn't smoked I would have been able to sleep.

I met new friends who lived quite close to me and began spending time with them. They smoked too, a lad and two lasses, but this however didn't last long. Another night of jerking alcohol and strong cannabis with grease food out of my system enabled me to stay away from them. But they were not the problem to my second failure that year; I again can only be blamed.

That term I was doing too much along with smoking extraordinary amounts. I was determined to give up once everything was well. How could smoking actually make a difference? I was sober the year prior for three whole months and I failed, thus smoking now in moderation should pass me this time as I can keep my head straight and away from guilt. There was no guilt just utter repentance that we didn't get to go to the seaside.

That season I found another job at a bar beside the River Thames; The Doggett's Coat and Badge, Bar and Restaurant. Here I worked most evenings and weekends. The bar had a brilliant atmosphere with tourist from around the world spending a little more than usual on a pint of lager and us getting paid a little less than usual for working. This wasn't a problem as all this was a charade for me to feel better about having a smoke in the evenings.

Why did my body crave this way of life? And how did I become so used to this? I felt remorse every-time I lit a joint, and when I was out of joints I really insisted on getting more even though I knew I will have regret once I did. But exams were the most important so stay calm and they will arrive and this constant odour will dissolve away once and for all. And round and round this thought circled as the days of winter turned to spring.

Spring came and I was arrested again, this being my second however on a heavier charge of drink driving. I had happened to be returning home from a club with five people who I chose to unload at their apartment and decided to take a short cut. Hundreds of people took this short cut over Blackfriar's Bridge but I happened to take the right turn with a police van hidden around the corner. There was no reckless driving involved as the road was clear and I was stable. The officer agreed that many take this turning however failing a Breathalyzer Test I lost my license for a year and all this before my finals, which were approaching slowly. To redeem myself from this I knew of a fantastic forget and carry on with life remedy and that was to begin smoking once more. Tanya happened to assist the friends home that night and waited till I was released from jail, and hence I felt obligated to Tanya for longer, thus spent more time with her and more time beside the green pot.

She smoked because I did and I used her presence to smoke further as she never complained. Nevertheless I'm sure if she had complained I would have spent more time at Weston Street smoking. Surely time drifted with me inside and I failed again. I knew I had failed once the exam was over and I waited to see the result in black and white. I called home to return again for three months to the South.

Back to England I lived at Weston Street Accommodation for a week and was asked to find another place due to car parking restrictions. I should have thought clearly at that time and moved to my relatives for three months. I will have this degree this time as I feel more reassurance that Jesus has forgiven me for my sins, so I'll work hard, smokeless, and satisfy my family and my teachers by succeeding on 9th November 2005. I found an apartment with parking ten minutes walking distance from university in London. At the time however I had never imagined that someone else had better plans for that date.

That apartment was leased by a huge hard breathing alcoholic landlord, Brian. He seemed kind enough to rent me the apartment; however I had no idea that he had dispute with his last tenant. Just to rectify I smoked during this season too. At this moment I was running thin of hair and out of patience for myself. Pot was the only thing that made me feel worthy and trying to leave this made me feel depressed and suicidal. I was not used to praying and especially after seven years now I couldn't afford to take a gamble. God knows I tried.

From September 2005 to November 2005 I was a victim of what Brian had suffered from with his last tenant. This tenant owed Brian money, this tenant had also broken into the apartment on the night I had moved in and had entered my room. I woke from sleep to find a shadow standing at the foot of my bed and once I blinked he had ran out with my jeans that were on the couch. I'm assuming he was hoping to find a wallet. This tenant after a month had come to the flat to check on his post and happily grinned when I asked him how my jeans fit. Before I could ask for them back and no involvement between him and the landlord he ran.

The landlord thought I had something to do with his break-in which I couldn't imagine why, but Brian ended up involving the rest of the tenants against me. An American girl, Margaret, helped Brian point fingers against me as she wasn't happy that the washing wasn't getting done and that there was a FHM in the toilet. Brian used the tenants to file a police order against me and sent a letter to the Dean of Guy's Hospital asking him to reframe from passing me until he received his money.

I had paid Brian a month's rent in advance plus more and decided to leave once my result was published. The Dean of Guy's Dentistry asked me to explain the situation and asked for me to stay away from the apartment. I agreed but not before I could clear my name with the flat-mates. I wrote a letter for Margaret to read out aloud to them and a man named Paul whom Margaret had invited to the reading. They became fully aware that my interest alone was to pass my exams and they apologized for their fault, and realized that I had no hand in whatever Brian suffered. The next morning was my final, final, final exam.

The exam ended with failure. With all the help I received from the doctors and the hope I felt from God I charted the teeth of a seven-year-old girl wrong. She was missing her adult lateral incisors and I concluded that they were already present in her mouth. I hadn't rectified my mistake in the final oral exam. At the time thought I had passed with flying colours. Throughout seven years I had never made such a mistake. Once the result was published I went to see the man in charge, he advised for me to appeal on the grounds of pressure induced by my landlord just prior to the exam. I declined.

All I felt was that I had enough; I couldn't face another failure like this again. This was a mistake, I should have appealed and taken another chance, another six months my parents could have afforded but at the time I felt that my parents would not be able to afford this, that I wasn't being fair on them and felt adamant on leaving things as they were and starting fresh in the United States.

I spoke to Mike once leaving the hospital that night. We drove to Leicester and smoked several blunts on the way. He smiled and agreed to my stubborn decision to forget and keep what was said that day a secret from everyone, except his mother. (Which was kept a secret from me until I returned back to England to stamp an American visa). Not saying the truth to Romeo once we got to Leicester and not saying anything to Vassell either, not letting anyone know and smoking passed the time for appeal faster than a fly fleeing from being squashed. It's not like Romeo didn't know that something was wrong. He knew I had sat my final exam, he knew of my behaviours and he knew I had failed.

How did everything become obscure was obvious, and when did I go wrong was not a matter anymore, but how was I to burn an eternity after maintaining faith in God for so long? I held hope in Jesus but I didn't stop smoking, people have their ways to rejoice after they lose and I chose to have nothing and no one except that given from narcotics and alcohol.

Today I live entirely for Him, like the King of Babylon Nebuchadnezzar after God released him from mad cow disease in the days of Judah's exile. However unlike Nebuchadnezzar I hadn't begun with atheism and thus my heart was more than flesh. And now after a seven-year reign from taking my oath to Bhagavan sitting in the Church of Christ S.C. He has made me realize why I was made to suffer. And for this I am thankful.

Part X

Ten

Build, build, build, stronger, stronger, heavier, heavier, last fireman alive in an earthquake and only one pound of meat left to save. I say to myself trying to lift more iron. Halle Berry eating a peach, Abhishek Bachchan eating a peach, Tom Cruise eating a peach. Worth saving, worth fighting for, worth being prepared. And all that remains is the creepy crawlies to work with our fertilizers and amino groups so we can grow more peaches.

Lift! Lift! Pull! Pull! Lift! Up! Down! Up! Down! Lift! Watch intensively and concentrate as we enjoy rain from our bodies grow peaches and red apples, anything else is not acceptable. Lights on and tiles mounted. Watch, turn, fill Gray's anatomy with colour, and watch Bruce Willis eating pineapple chunks, and accept the best, and accept nothing without the Lord's love and nothing less than that.

This is my flesh and my flesh will purify the earth and the atmosphere, and I shall fill every ounce of muscle tissue with nutrient so after my soul is snatched from my flesh, my flesh will not poison His Earth. Do as the mercenaries before us and I shall be rewarded with the eternal life. Help as the mercenaries before us. Boast the word of the Spirit and boast in righteousness so the will of our existence be appreciated every day.

"CLEAR! CLEAR!"

"Beep, beep."

"We have a pulse."

Through the arch and down the escalator just in time for the silver tubing to take me home. I love Lara Mosum. And she loves me. Not just your average thinks she loves to love, but like Whitney Houston that has my love and your love and Lara's love, Lara Mosum orbiting around Jupiter's love.

There she is with her car waiting to check out her man, who is purposefully trying not to bump into people on his way out of the station. Thanking the cleaner at Waterloo and showing him a dirt spot on the ceiling, I walked to her and embraced. I had just come back from answering a high school class across the pond a silly question like what to do if someone faints.

"Did you end up showing any senior students how to respond?" she asked.

"Not until we sit down love, that was a long flight, and I watched all the movies that were on, and at every commercial looked out the window, and then I tried to close my eyes to pretend I was sleeping, but I actually fell asleep. And now here I am with an empty belly and my mouth open," I replied.

We embraced. Well she embraced most of that one, I was too busy watching the cars, and black cabs, and the life filtering into me from London and a red bus came to a stop just as she finished.

The time was just past nightfall and a hint of light could be seen from the west corner of our way home. Clearly she helped with the bags curious with what I forgot to throw away. We had a relationship where I would not buy her anything; she was the only reason for which I wanted to see her. And I stuck by it and through our time away from each other nothing was bought. I bought a tie for myself and a shirt for my mate. Nothing wrong with buying your best mate a car if you could I think.

I love flowers and He loves birds, she loves anything we love as we love her. And He loves her diva, who loves Him and Whitney Houston who I still think loves everyone. And then we went to eat.

Eleven

rrepientanse," I said whilst turning away a cigarette. "*Arrepientanse, porque el reino de los cielos esta cerca. Mateo tres: cuatro*. And I am glad to repent on the past. I can't believe I was called fruit-cake by everyone from ninth to twelfth grade," I said.

"Don't forget the girls called you that as well. Good job you threw that ass out the window. Priceless, still amazes me how you knew the glass would break," said Huliyo.

Huliyo was my best friend since I moved to The City of Leicester Secondary School; he came to my home every morning and we walked to school. We happened to swap porn from twelve, but no one can love a girl better than Huliyo's brother.

"I repent on not spending more time with you at college," burped Huliyo.

"I repent that I tried to date girls at college and didn't offer to share. I'm sorry."

"I'll drink to that!"

And welcome back to the ninety-eighth lap of the first week in July 2008, here at Daytona and a fantastic day we are having. The road is nice and warm so the drivers have plenty of grip to pull smooth tractions. When night falls anything could happen as the roads start to cool down and more focus from the drivers have to be driven.

Nascar. Daytona. 2008.

"I also appreciate how Jesus Christ showed me the way to every man's heart as seriously I would have killed him. For four years he smiled and on a return visit he greats me with all curses made from hell," I began.

"Yes I'm glad that someone finely placed some sense into you. But next time let us not go to a party and begin repenting," Huliyo forwarded, "makes me want to cry on some blonde girl's bosom because I have never been able to do that."

"Sometimes what troubles me is that I wish Jesus came to my life sooner. Maybe I would have been able to read for the will of learning sooner."

"And maybe you could have explored further on how to travel at light speed," sarcastically replied Huliyo.

"I would have arrived well on Moni and would not have become seduced by temptations if the Father came sooner," I said whilst watching the bar maid rub past Frank the bar manager.

"Yes. Well that is neither here or there, and who knows what would have happened between Craig lover and you," slugged Huliyo. "Just be glad that you chose to save yourself when you did. And I thank my Saviour for you too."

"What I don't repent on is explaining to people that Christ is not by nationality but our deliverance on accepting that the Lord is eternal. My God people that speak different languages find it difficult to accept that my walk, my talk and my strike a nail is by believing good for all people. I wish I was white," I continued.

"Again with you wishing you were different colours. How come you cannot be happy with how you are? That's a monkey with two testicles, what more could you want?" Huliyo poured himself come ice-tea and sat back to watch the barmaid stare at a customer's necklace.

"Can we get some nachos with meat and salsa?" I asked Frank.

"So decided to get married, have some children, hope you don't start repenting on them too now," laughed Huliyo. "Go and take a ride."

"Don't be stupid, every early morning I may have to repent. Especially if the season is on, I may as well start repenting now. And for my children they will repent on their death," I smiled whilst Carl Edwards knocked Jeff Gordon out of the race.

"Whoa! Did you see that? Oh another one! I hope they are all fine," I looked over at Huliyo's brain with a puzzled look. And looking at the screen he said: "I have a wager with him next week and without the good odds the pay off will be lousy."

"Well if you do win some money then I need a couple of grand for a birthday party," I asked.

"Sure," he said whilst digging into the hot plate of nachos and minced brisket with cool salsa sauce splayed all over.

"Fine I'll eat to that," I said whilst digging into the hot plate of nachos and minced brisket with cool salsa sauce splayed all over.

Twelve

First week of freshman year went according to what was on the menu. A bar at the halls and a 12-foot snooker table to accompany passing time on at King's College Hall, located at Denmark Hill on the south-eastern rail lines for Greater London. Every morning we would walk down the hill to the station, and then back again to bed or the bar. If Hansel and Gretel didn't come to play then this would be a different story.

Christmas was spent in Leicester as Short Stuff had plans to organize a party and nothing was better than witnessing his smile let alone any party, with any selection of laughs and places to let down and dwell, than the parties that Short Stuff held. The new year of 1998 was spent well with the family too.

Back to King's College Hall and spending mostly all the time reading or consolidating with the girls what other girls like. And other times with the lads to organize a plan on how to reign as kings. No anger and no tension expressed when living away from home, no exposure to unkindness and no repentance anymore as this was the time to succeed, socially as well as academically.

Who will be the strongest leader in the pack? And how strong will they make the pack? That was the only thing in my mind when leaving Wyggeston and Queen Elizabeth I College, and clearing a section away from bullying and into civilization. The motto on my book bag read, "If you can't speak civil then best to get out!" And I had that bag for the entire period at King's College.

The first day of classes was by waiting for my friend outside McDonald's and walking to the lecture hall together. After that day she made friends and I made friends. And we lived in separate halls until the third year of our course.

"I believe in love, I believe in love, Shabba, Shabba. Shabba believes in love, must respect the blood, and must not shed blood. It's a family affair; it's a family affair. I care, do you care, if you care put your han'y han'y in the air, and clap them load and clear."

Shabba Ranks. Family Affair. 1993.

The second year was spent slowly at a friend's who I personally loved. This guy was cool, and spoke well and read just as well as I. He happened to have less practice speaking native Gujarati at home but he was well witted in speaking what was practical and fair. I loved him, and he loved my girlfriend, who loved me, so we lived happily ever after that year.

The first day I moved into his apartment we went to drink at the local pub. The rest of that year went on drilling and spraying false teeth on phantom heads. We arrived home every night after digging into our books and toning into our muscles the will of God to enjoy repenting with a Kronenbourg, in a Foster's glass at The Old Nag.

"So when's your girlfriend coming back to visit?" asked my flatmate Patel.

"She should be coming anytime soon, she says she misses you, and cannot wait to see how much you have lost weight," I replied.

"So your girlfriend has started checking me out. More brains and brawn, then money, and then I will be able to buy a girlfriend as luscious as yours."

"You can have her, but only once you qualify, otherwise we are both done for."

"What do you mean?" asked Patel.

"Do you know that there are so many girls and that they are all the same? Meaning that the only way to find true love is through the Lord, so if you desire perfection you must be willing to sign your will," I replied.

"What? So she is like the spider that kills her mate for offspring and I'm her mate?" he asked.

"Well I know you believe in *Espiritu Santo* so your soul is safe with whoever you try and catch in your web, but if she worships the devil then don't make me say I told you so. Why don't you start taking that swimmer out instead of thinking about my girlfriend?"

"Man, I'm going to miss you next year, not living with you and all. Make sure to say hi to me everyday man," Patel continued.

"You sit beside me everywhere I go, what if I too wish to talk about boobies will you concur?" I asked.

"Sure I would. Are you thinking amplitude or wavelength?" he laughed to himself.

The remaining three years disappeared as fast as they had arrived. I happened to move to a more affordable flat and one that happened to be closer to university. I lived with a girl and a guy, but was mostly on the phone to Lara. If the phone had not rang then time at the flat would be spent in the kitchen or in the guy's room.

Ronald was my flat-mate and a keen learner in chemistry. He enjoyed cooking and happened to be a crewmember for Selfridges' kitchen on Oxford Street. He cooked for his family and friends on his twenty-first, and he cooked for me when Lara came to visit.

Gabrielle lived with us too; she was hardly at home as she spent time with her books and with people who enjoyed reading rather than those that enjoyed eating and sitting on the porcelain throne. Her time at the flat was either for laundry or for a break from her "study" partner and those times were great. We three ate, laughed and went to bed early after a cold shower.

Three years went by with us coming in and out of Redman House, and music bellowed from times of flat cleansing. I could not have asked for better flat-mates. Ronald had a tendency to keep things clean and tidy, and Gabrielle would blow a fit if there were no clean plates. When I was at the flat time was spent taking naps in the afternoon, reading, mastering the latest version of EA sports on the Playstation and of course the phone.

"I love the way your girlfriend holds her thong on her waist," said Ronald one day, "do you think you can ask your girlfriend to have a word with my girlfriend so I don't have to always check your girl out?" he asked.

"Now, now, why don't you ask her yourself?" I said whilst we prepared dinner on a winter night.

"Do you think I want my girlfriend to feel jealous? If I wanted to frustrate her I would look at her forehead with my puzzled look," he said whilst giving me the same gesture.

"Well I'll speak to her, and do you want me to ask her to wear Liverpool stripes too?" I asked sarcastically.

"Hmmm. Not yet. Just ask her to ask Mary to show some lace on the side once in a while that's all I ask," Ronald insisted.

"I'll ask her to ask Mary to wear and show lace. Now you know that they will start shopping together and begin to become best of friends. And at your age do you really want that?" I asked him.

"Okay just the thongs, sometimes on the right, sometimes on the left, not really in the center and no synchronizing clocks, that's all I ask," he paused whilst opening a bottle of red. "I know you can place it discretely to her, so in your own time but preferable for tomorrow's walk to the Eye."

"I will be as discrete on your kinky issues as Mickey Mouse looking at Minnie's legs, but how would you like The Thong to discretely mention it to Mary?" I suggested.

"Let me think about it for a while," he hummed whilst he drained the pasta. "I got it. You ask Miss Thong which side she prefers wearing the thong at dinner tonight, then ask her if all girls prefer that same side and then switch to Mary to ask her," Ronald smuggled like a mad scientist coming to a conclusion.

"Got it, then she will say that she doesn't show her thongs and that is when you ask her that she should, especially tomorrow when we go to the Eye."

"That's brilliant!" he said, and began drinking ahead of me to gain the Dutch courage that was needed for this spin. "If all back fires, then two tears in a bucket…"

"Yes this is London and there are a million other girls to choose from. I love living here."

"Ya, and I will love you if you don't forget about this," he replied, and the doorbell rang.

Thirteen

University was a trip, just as we finished we drank, as we always did, drink and breathe in passive hand smoking. (Important bridges built my fair lady). As graduates we assumed that someone will collapse on that night, and a bar full of certified doctors who will be the first guinea pig and who will come to the rescue? Through Carlsberg, Stella, Jack Daniels, Gin, Vodka and a mix array from where we were that night could not have ever been better.

"Wanna say, wanna say, wanna say, yaaaa! Ya!" I said.

"What's up? What's uuup?" blurred Naomi.

"Well it's not your hand down my pants this time," I proclaimed.

"Can I drink more?" asked my love.

"Smack down, two bottoms up and three men in a tub," I said and the drinks refilled.

"I'm bad! I'm bad! You know, I'm bad. When the whole world tries to answer my question I tell you once again, who's bad?!!"
Michael Jackson. Bad. 1987.

Looking back at everything from moving for the first time to the time of deliverance all I wanted to do that night was sleep. Sit back, watch a movie and thank God that I was chosen to help. Like David Beckham, this blade of grass Sir! This one with the ant looking for a fine opportunity. *Dichosos Jesucristo.*

"Let's all jump around, all jump around!" I shouted after jugging a large one against the one arrogant Bangladeshi I knew of class '98, (a dear friend whom I was not there for much and hope that the height of this cliff be enough to keep us from missing the missed opportunities).

"What do you mean jump around?" and Mr. Bangladeshi started bouncing on the spot.

"This is what it should be like every day," I said.

"Oh you're just saying that as you are drunk and I am bouncing on the spot as I am drunk," returned Mr. Bangladeshi.

He celebrated his moment of sincerity into the floor of bouncing heads, and snapping thongs, and black cabs *y nuestro harmano*.

"I know this is going to sound stupid, but … Ha! Ha! Ha!" came falling into the circle of pillars, by the bar, away from an ashtray, the one and only lad that brought Jesus into everyday conversation. "Am I still born one month after Jesus?" Anthony asked.

"Yes," we replied.

"I don't know who to make out with anymore; both wanting an opening and now they want it again," he staggered to call the waitress for a drink and to be kind enough to ask the D.J. to change the track. "What is it going to be like when I'm rich? Who shall I buy?" asked Anthony.

"Penelope Cruz!" I replied. "That is if I needed someone to keep my apartment clean, but considering I have crazy Mosum to keep all things warm I'd have to run it past her," I said whilst my words caught up to my own thought.

"Yes, filling cavities, one for money and the other to burn money. Life cannot become better than that," Mr. Bangladeshi returned.

"All I need in this life of sin is me and my girlfriend."

Jay Z ft Beyonce. Me and My Girlfriend. 2002.

That night was smashing and now time for the men to have some fun. "Who is up for Chinese?" I asked a group of fairly well alcohol-tolerated individuals that were clutching onto each other as the night air of London filled our intoxicated blood.

"Walk, walk, walk, walk... Walk, walk, walk," chanted the girls as they grabbed onto one another through Leicester Square into Soho, and onto wooden chairs, around a wooden table, with wooden chopsticks and amongst busy speaking Chinese persons.

That night we ate much slower than any other that we had shared. Food kept arriving to the table, and the men from us ate as well as did some girls and across three hours the diner began to fall asleep.

"Wine! We need wine," He claimed, clang, clang, clang. "A toast, a toast to us all," He forwarded.

"*Gan bei!*" I said.

"*Gan bei!*" we all said.

"Amen," we then all spoke of, and stepped out of Mr. Lee's restaurant into a brighter morning.

If anything could have made that day better then that would be to love and read this passage again, again, again and again.

After B.C.

Fourteen

Screech, went the wheels on the bus, the wheels on the bus, the wheels on the bus. Screech, went the wheels on the bus my Lord. What?! Three rounds of acres on my left and three rounds of acres on my right, watch the south as I know you had something to do with that. All my prays and you take that one? That was the pray that you chose for me to share with you as you are well Almighty? Why you did this I know. You keep beating me to the checker flag as the position for evil is up for sale.

A year into programmed saved life and I wish Jesus had come sooner. Thanks for showing me that righteousness was a way to live and that I was right! I had been denying my acceptance with existence for so long until I agreed to read Scripture in English. There were things in the world, a word, a sentence written as law to help me understand the way of life. This helped me dumb my life a little.

Kudha ki bhala, Aqbar ki dooha, chose shipment of goods across borders before He praised someone who cries only for a stranger. Father where for are you so I can show you that I can stand? Where are you so I can show that I fell and laughed as I am crazy to do it again? Almost lost you in 2001 A.D. makes me laugh, I thought I was asking to be saved by someone who has been worshipped for eternity, not be victimized by the second and third class American citizen as they prone me to do something worse.

Queen Elizabeth II's chauffer would be in hysterics if exposed to driving here. Where the land is vastly open and valleys are as far as the eyes can see, greed bubbles on the tarmac and mostly boils freely. Five acres ahead the chauffer can see the golden arches of McDonald's where he would have his eye on. Unlike the Queen who would have her frown eye on several robots climbing tail in mouth up the valley and closely closing in was your local friendly neighbourhood cop with no emergency except to observe why he too should not have a tail in his mouth. She laughs, she cries and she just decides to throw her knickers out the window. She must make me laugh when I see this as for sure now I will kill.

I happened to be fortunate in one year; one arrest for resisting arrest, three speeding tickets, two negligent driving tickets, and one ticket for having a beginner's permit and only one I can say that full blame fell on my disobedience. I thank you Lord for showing me the world of sin and now I know that was the same world that I just grew out of, nevertheless this world's people file for treason. Without you Jesus I would not have entered the United States, I can only praise your existence as without you I would have only seen rotten degrading hearts under blindingly polished golden badges, and I would have taken a whole warehouse full of vampires to hell for my children.

The resisting arrest began as a police officer could not understand how a British-Indian dude could freely speak to Blacks (African-Americans) in the suburbs of U.S. 25 South Carolina. I had just moved to South Carolina and I wished for nothing more than a tall bridge. Instead the Lord's right hand grabbed me, and punched me, and threw me on to the floor and into a cell after making my family spend three grand on a MRI at the local hospital.

I was with friends drinking until the officer forces authority for I to sit indoors and him to provide neighbourhood watch. I became blamed by the Blacks for speaking to the officer and decided to leave, where the officer now decides he too wishes to find out why I came back out of the home I was asked to go back into.

Now do I wish for the Blacks to think ill as I am not Black or a White cop to help me sober? Maybe I was asking for too much but at the time I acted on impulse and decided to leave. I pulled to a stop around the corner and got out the car to catch air. The cop follows and begins to arrest me, before I can ask why I was thrown on my car and beaten from above. I spent the rest of the first year placing community service to clear my name.

Welcome to America, yes the land of the brave. What everyone hears around the world is that America is united, the place to live and so we are, thanks to *Allah*, and thanks to this cop that he decided to hit Christ and not someone that could not afford the government's greedy charges including health costs!

Three thousand dollars for an MRI at Greenville Memorial Hospital and no antiseptic, yes I get it, you're American and I am not. I am just another shit taker in your systematic shit-taking nation. "Imitate I, as I imitate Christ." That is what Apostle Paul said to the Corinthians to explain the word of Jesus Christ around 100 A.D. I walked back into the Christian school with a bruised face first week of term still not aware that I am too Christ. A year of money well earned spilt into a corrupt government, the people are corrupt but they are at no more faults than the government or was it just another one idiot?

I have strength as I am black and in a tie. Into the Pre-Trial Intervention program where my advisor couldn't understand that an Indian could speak English better than his slave father and wished to pin mental asylum for me. He couldn't understand where I just came from and where I was going; instead he wished to stab me further with more costs. Only when I asked for another advisor my PTI program came to a close, and my name supposedly became cleared and gained the right again to live in America for my family.

Surprising I still had my sense of humour. I disappointed my family by failing at King's College London, and now in the first month of student visa-ship I have a criminal record. Amen to the crows. Amen to the officer, but restriction to the hospital who without consent on that night became as careless as I who fell for Jesus' sorrow.

Another ticket from a greedy, stupid, lucky; young officer that took his book of oath to stapling a speeding ticket whilst I was blinking to turn a left ninety. There was another who wished to ticket for a right blinking ninety. For what the English men would say is an indication to turn, i.e. for you to slow down or stop. Not to speed up and force a ticket. Give one Indian a careless ticket and face extreme Islamists at judgment. Face extreme Indians at judgment. Amen. Meet me and you will not have time to say your name before I send you to one of the twenty-eight planets of hell. Amen.

I try to remind myself that not all government officials are bad, not all U.S. citizens are bad, but they are all stupid. If one man cannot physically make things better then why does he marry? Why not adopt children than breed insecure ones? In a nation that has everything from each end of the Earth the people live like barbarians, wanting to fight with their tin cars that mine is bigger than yours and later smile superficially at the local gas stations like men in black and I'm an evil alien. Ha! The American teens are forced to drive around with fear in their hearts as men shadow with trucks and women with blood diamonds speed dial for more corrupt officers. Ha!

Unlike Jesus I had to built faith in the Father to cure teenagers erupted by acne/leprosy from fear due to who would sue and who would pursue. I advice waiting for the sufferer to look at ones lips to reduce anxiety levels of fear from one another by one looking at their lips when waiting for a burger at a drive-thru window. Catch my drift?

"... the law says, it says to those ... under the law, so ... every mouth ... silenced and the whole world held accountable to God. Therefore no one ... righteous in God's sight by the works of the law; rather, through the law we ... conscious of our sin. But now apart from the law the righteousness of God has been made known, to which the Law & the Prophets testify."   [Romans 3:19-21]

One more ticket by an officer who springs a 180 degree turn across a median to catch me as I had a clear road on 65mph. So he had his mouth around someone's tail. Lucky shit! I paid tickets and extra costs and my father paid the depression for Jesus, and these so-called modern Christians, troop savers, whatever should remember the day they prophesized to kill poor Mr. Liberty's son; if you drive too close then someone somewhere is bound to get hurt.

Quick phone call and the police again are on my tail. Stupid idiots do not observe the caller for tailing instead listen only to the caller and home all on me as I steadily drive on the right of a two-lane road. Please catch up to me when you drive, lick my ass and kiss it as you have no tendency to rub alcohol on the U.S. Army tag, but to drink instead and try to spark my fuse. Thank someone that Jesus got to me sooner than the devil, the devil that everyone in the world was afraid of and that Jesus that saved some of U.S. finest state troopers.

Later two neglecting driving tickets: One was for driving with my left leg out the window. Not on the phone whilst driving, not with a dog on my lap, or your kid, or a child or a police officer with a gunshot wound to the hospital asking the left to be clear, but for driving slowly on the right on a hot day minding my own business for a Greenville cop to pull me over in traffic. This one was a thousand dollars. I had my leg out the window, morality of her decision was wrong. Keep your eye on the road not at depressed me. Now, now that ticket I deserved, nevertheless it was a really hot week. This I would regard as the ticket I deserved. I suffered another three months to plead innocent, plead a sorry, and mention I was a student. The fine was dropped to four hundred and that almost wrapped a year in the United States.

From where I just came from thank God for drugs, as only with drugs I coped with family, study, work, America, friends and memories.

Just into the last year of Southern Wesleyan University S.C. and the other ticket was on the horizon and filed for driving negligently to school. I apprehended my speed to make way for another person and ended up moving behind them as they were clearly in a rush. So much rush that they had time to call the police as they found righteousness unwelcoming to the tarred heart they possessed, and with no proof Officer Maria, awarded me with a ticket for negligent driving outside the school zone all thanks to a quick phone call.

Now across one year and nothing had been kept constant in my life but my patience with the Lord so I tempt Him to make another suffer for liberty. A week passes and a church bus for Picken's topples killing an adolescent man from S.C. 93 Liberty School, and the bus driver. I still cry for his father, I still will not stop for this system and I will still pray for his father.

Again that clearly may have not been associated with me, but when I stole a Superman trademark keychain just for Christopher Reeves to have peace some spirits overheard and stuck a little more closely.

"Above all, you must understand that no prophecy of Scripture came about by the prophet's own interpretation of things. For prophecy never had its origin in the human will, but prophets, though human, spoke from God as they were carried along by the Holy Spirit." [2Peter 1:20-21]

"POLICEMAN'S PRAYER: Archangel Michael, Heaven's glorious Commissioner of Police, who once so neatly and successfully cleared God's premises of all undesirables, look with a kindly and professional eye on your earthly force. Give us cool heads, stout hearts, hard punches, an uncanny flair for investigation, and wise judgement. Make us the terror of burglars, the friend of children and law-abiding citizens, kind to strangers, polite to bores, strict with law-breakers, and impervious to temptations. You know, St. Michael, from your own experiences with the devil, that the policeman's lot on Earth is not always a happy one; but your sense of duty that so pleased God, your hard knocks that so surprised the devil, and your angelic self-control give us inspiration. And when we lay down our night sticks, enrol us in your Heavenly Force, where we will be as proud to guard the throne of God, as we have been to guard the city of men. Amen."

Fifteen

The decision to move to America came from the conference table across the Gopal family wood set at the old house in Leicestershire. My father's brothers had decided to move to North Carolina moving the business of textiles into closure and setting home in the New World with their families during the first years of the second millennium. Their children would attend American schools and they themselves would facilitate hotel management across the eastern shore of America. I really had enjoyed my company when I was with them. From youth they were the ones organising outings and group dinners. They came to play with me when my father was away and they attended my parents evening. Pity a lot was made to change. But the most important thing was that they are still there.

My father was to remain behind to coordinate the last closures of the two-decade business in England, my mother to help and my sister to begin packing and being accustomed to moving a year earlier than them. The best interest towards my sister's education would be for her to move much sooner than the rest of us.

She moved to South Carolina as my *masi's* (mum's sister's) family had moved to America from India to the South a year prior to my sister's move. Her, her two children and her husband became fortunate in God's grace to move to South Carolina and present a new life for themselves away from India.

I could not imagine much difference in the culture changes compared to England and the States but my cousins endorsed difficulty. I had no worry about my sister's move, she spent one year with *masi's* family, and attended school and weekly phone calls kept me reassured that she was doing much better in the States than previously at home.

From all my cousins one was a girl a couple of years older than my sister, and one was a lad a couple of more years older than her. The phone calls were answered mostly by my sister as she was the one mostly at home; she kept in her studies, gymnastics, and waiting to buy her car, and waiting for us whilst doing her nails.

That season I was in London at Redman House in anticipation on moving to the States myself. Times became difficult as waiting to ensure the wellbeing of my sister became more long winded. Finish exams was the only thing on my cards, to finish them well became obsolete and time was spent more by wasting time rather than following in the work of Jesus Christ.

A year from this date passed and I had failed entry to the exams at Guy's Hospital, and more months of practice were needed to reassure the promise of graduating in the next season.

"Let us go in peace!" said my father before they left for S.C. in August 2004.

That was the last thing I heard my father say as I moved to Norbury for a hopeful season to pass in the winter of 2004. Just as my father could predict my best, I carried to work and they formulated living quarters with my *masi's* family.

The distance between what was an empire of a family in Leicestershire had dissolved and stretched a couple of hours across I-85, and love was further away from us including my participation in the family's happiness. Was this the reason why Jesus chose to save my life as I cared for others over myself, or is that everything in the Bible is true including Jesus who would save those who sincerely ask for him? Acceptance to ask for judgment on my life and wipe the slate clean on the other came more and more apparent as my purpose in life became meaningless.

False smiles and courteous handshakes to maintain the good spirit of my mother's conscious with her new life members in South Carolina, and forgiving appraisals for my father's side isolation agenda. My move to the States strongly pulsed in my blood as I waited season after season, failure after failure, just to try and make things right. To find purpose in my life and association with my descending family line happened to become more apparent as time ticked in my life in England. Everyone wants me to pass dentistry, I want to pass, and move to the States, pass again in the States, and qualify as a professional across two nations and find peace within the universe.

Time drifted still and everyone grew older. My *kaka's* children hopefully have forgotten what had happened and have become strong American residencies. My sister who I knew would not have peace until she sees my safety would need reassurance that things would be okay. For her life was different. She spoke with whatever tone she wished and said whatever was necessary and not even a scolding or a abrupt stop. Because of her and moving to the States my parents opened up to the modern way of living. Pity it was too late to find ways to love me.

A long time ago before a time can be made their lived kings. A prophet of the Lord was named

Samuel and he anointed Saul to become king
before David. David was asked to work by Saul
until the Lord called for David to be king. King
David filled with repentance through his years of
adultery, murder and betrayal of his son's sword
finished writing his apologies on his always aging
deathbed. Through the king repenting he was
delivered to the Promise Land, regardless of when
he was a king at his best or worst.

When time had reached the present I had
endorsed enough from neglecting myself from life,
and had enough from pessimistic remarks without
any truth from the thousands of righteous people I
had encountered including my parents. Remarks
were well given to do my best and not to worry,
however I had no worry, I consumed my life with
drugs, alcohol and wrong desires to find no
purpose to move to the straight and narrow.

I found the straight and narrow and this was
to overcome the sinful. People filled with ignorant
arrogance. Those that had been blessed with a
silver platter but would always be compelled to
speak rather than to listen, those that would
interrupt others' sentences, those like my mother,
my father and I. No need for you to speak when I
can counteract your comment. And when trying to
speak to my parents I never was able to finish a
sentence. Painfully I found myself; painfully I
began to forgive my parents.

Christ gave me strength that God, our Father was standing beside me and to help me finish my sentences. The art was to carrying on the sentence through interruption. I would begin to speak whilst the other would begin to speak their own. Speak over their sentence, not stopping just because they had started speaking. I would finish my sentence whilst listening to theirs; wait for them to finish and then comment on their remark.

I found the shameful would not be able to comprehend the speech pattern with sincerity for the other i.e. they would become jealous before enlightened. The innocent would become enlightened to speak. Multiple conversations in the same time of space is not unusual; sparrows perched in trees speak in this tongue, so if birds could do that without biting each other so could I.

Overall unless I was singing I preferred enjoying others company in silence. With this I noticed that the usual insults came from those that thought they had something to prove around the clock. Foreigners to the will of God would speak suited to their ego, loud and in haste instead of slowly and clearly. Makes me laugh that some would try to please themselves rather than our Father. Nonetheless speak *lentamente y claramente.*

"How attractive and beautiful they will be! Grain will make the young men thrive, and new wine the young women." [Zechariah 9:17]

Now having the confidence to speak I needed to bite back. The pity was that I was biting back at my parents; I needed to find what was keeping me alive, why did I wish to live longer when the cliff was at my toes to fall from? I learnt a little too late on how to accept standing on my own two feet. I wish my mother had not rebelled against my father and her in-laws, I wish I had not rebelled against him; I wish he hadn't encouraged my rebellion. Nevertheless I needed to move away from the life I suffered in England to find approval for my disapproval for the ones I loved. I needed to either move then or not at all.

I thank my Lord, I thank my Lord to help me hold my tears, I wait for my Lord, now I wait for my Lord closer to home. Help me Lord and help me find purpose in my love for others. Help me, help me smile again; make me understand the reason why forgiveness is painful. Make me understand why I was born under the sun and all my days of drifting I have found no peace except in your name and only in your name I am happy to suffer. If no room in the world to suffer in Your name allow me to create my own Lord to explain my suffering, and the reason for the dozens of crows flying King James Tri-quetra over my head.

Sixteen

The history of the United States had come much earlier in my life. The history of my first flight with vomits into a bag, onto the floor of a yellow cab, through something or other and out for the last time across the world at the age of six. From New York, to San Francisco, to Las Vegas and on the second sitting Chicago and Houston. A time after that with the whole cavalry to Orlando and then an in-law wedding in Houston where I met for the first time the pressures of Texas police. Luckily nothing as close to the brutality of my first visit to S.C. no dent, no foul.

Houston, Hurricane Hut. The very first night out with my cousin and with his cousins on his dad's side, and one friend who we named *Khalnayak* from that night on as he happened to get arrested from a dozen lads.

"Two dollars a shot x," I said whilst reading this off a waitress's cleavage instead of leaving as one cousin was asked to leave as I asked him to hold my drink. *Khalnayak* walks in to call me out. Ha! And accused of trespassing and into the hard-earned tax dollar made car he went. A practicing *swami*, a well-respected boy in the community that night into a cell to spend the night. I obviously had no idea with what happens in the States, and their policies, plus I'm drunk and I have immaturity pumping through my blood. Jesus! With Her Majesty and the right to at least be slightly comprehensive I spoke to the officer.

"He's all ready left and will spend the night in the cell," the officer said.

In England that means: night in the cell and out in the morning, no charge. Disgraced when I hurt about bail and bond, and criminal records that can stick from a weak police enforcement system or an atheist ass!

So then on one arm my cousin is moving me back to the car and on the other using my height as an advantage cursing the pig's judgment. Right then from behind came another officer as fast as his engines could carry him and next thing I know I'm pinned to the side of my tax dollar. He searched and my cousins explained I was from England and I must be jet lagged, the officer asked me to calm down or he's placing me in for the night too.

Whoa! I asked to see his gun and that was the first night. Spent the night in the car till morning and a wire transaction back in time for *toda harmanas* to make us breakfast.

Harmano desegregation after Fredrick Douglas that Martin got shot, someone else got shot, and maybe JFK got shot because he was white and not religious. Whatever the reason was may be good job he did as I'm sure he would not have imagined what had come next. Sandwiches in lunch boxes thousands of feet in the air, a philistine bar with six butt cracks having lunch. The crow tips a cup and the cup dissolves to gravity. The only possibility I can suggest about closing this madness is by trying to show the groups of murderers a joy in sports.

Maybe a freedom trooper could bag a terrorist, bring him to the States and we'll go to watch a ball game. Once joy comes into his heart we would bag him back to never land. Pray and hope to have tears in our eyes as our children grow and compete in soccer matches, baseball matches, football matches, hockey matches, and 100-meter sprint dashes or just with plain dominos. What do we then do with a hundred thousand troops? We move them to African soil and build fridge doors that close to store the abundant amounts of food the earth offers for hundred or more so years.

On the other hand I could work harder and afford to knock something into the Taj Mahal.

There is plenty of rubble to make another one. Or the Black Stone of Mecca at the right timing might stop thousand vaginas mating for the sake of mating. Hence allow men to think how I too could come and touch the Black Stone and cry to say I can. Better still kill the shanty developers and have land to graze rabies free cattle. Just a suggestion like many others floating around my head.

Another maybe just eat and share cheeseburgers, who doesn't really like cheeseburgers? Nutrient and energy dense, plus in surplus supply unlike elephants, yes? If not, eat poultry, eat fish, eat potatoes and if you choose not to eat then sleep. Yawn! Dream about English Persians. Smile. If there was anything on earth that represents heaven then why not test the Lord to see if heaven's better?

"The coolest people in the world go to exercise!" Chant graduates watching a trashcan topple due to the wind on a hill that they were on and wonder what they could do better. The harsh story faces opinion; do we do better or not? We all have to die, so does the Indonesian grandmother who prays to Christ in what I can only gather as Arabic. Dissimilarly does the Indonesian grandmother's girlfriend imagine moving two years into darkness with authorization for me to take out Greenville Tech with my sister inside?

What I say does not matter considering what I have done. A night in the first month of S.C. and

I'm smoking patiently with the driver's door open. The car was parked in an open shopping car park as the U.S. have plenty of there. Two shadows appeared from behind my view.

"Give me your wallet!" said a voice.

"Okay, hold on," I said and got out my seat.

Before I had assessed the situation I had already had decided I had nothing to lose. I looked at a young African-American pointing a gun at me. He had his lips covered with his coat and so had his friend. I looked at him, then I look at his gun, then I looked at his friend, and then back to him. I had two choices, one being to step to the left and mark his head into the door frame of my car, and not checking for pulse, or:

"I'm a Police Officer; don't you think you should join the Army? Make a better living. Get out of here," I had said in my accent.

They were startled, said sorry, and left leaving me to carry on my smoke.

"It was now about the sixth hour, and darkness ... until the ninth hour, for the sun stopped shining. And ... curtain of the temple was torn in two. Jesus called out in a loud voice, "Father, into your hands I commit my spirit." ... breathed his last. ... centurion ... praised God and said, "Surely this was a righteous man." ... those who ... stood at a distance, watching these things."

[Luke 23:44-49]

I am of Christ, I am not white, I am not black, I am not yellow, I am not brown and I am not a zombie. Through Christ I will read and through *Allah* I will work. And through my knowledge I will boast as if I boast I will boast only about the Lord. Through whatever I look like, I too wish to boast about the Lord. Stamp me on a fifty star pole with my hands nailed back so I can watch my Lord day and night.

What more I learnt from "settling in" was that the Confederate Flag is the strongest flag I have seen in my life, from Dukes of Hazzard to the confused people in the world trying to stay calm through the burning heat of the east and the frost of the altitude. Find red things in prison, find red things in prison, and with good behaviour we would do over time! We will work out in prison and we will work out again!

Following into work at the gas station came following a creep one day. He followed me from bad driving and I stood waiting for him to park and complain. Standing in front of a black insulator tape stretched into a crucifix the creep instantly transformed into a man. I kept calling him a girl whilst he walked back to his car, but the truth was now he was neither man nor woman but an eternal light source.

Helping redeem soldiers and police officers during all hours of the day at a 24-hour gym totalled me to strengthen myself for the word of

God. I would pull iron and read the Holy Bible with flies that would sit alongside my thumb and read along with me.

"Quick! Quick! Hurry the plane is taking off!" I'd say to myself and jump onto the crow bar to pull myself into the open hatch. "One for you, one for him, one for her, one for them," I said lifting heavier pieces of iron in preparation for holding my own cross.

The old man says nothing as he waits pruning his weeds and mowing his farm, teaching his children how to build a sandcastle on a mountain. I adapted to this way of thinking for keeping myself calm across the transition period. I prayed for Jesus to save my life and if He had not I would not have cared much about any land or anybody.

So I begged for mercy in 2005, I begged for acceptance in 2000 and not until 2007 I realized that the only person I had to forgive was Jesus. Jesus forgave me and all my sins and everything I had lost, everyone I had inspired and every soul I thought not worthy of catching I left to fall far away from me. Forgave him again.

Maybe the Lord had grown weary and tired, and His own time of arrival was right for everyman. Southern Wesleyan students are better than the faculty and if you are not from true South then you will never understand the spells of Cottage Hill. Truth be told that the life of faith was recited over and over, in Scripture and as life until life became alive. Analyzing that with a scientific stand point I thought to measure Jesus by weighing faith with discipline. People that speak in Christ will enter a glorified life here as well as the other. Whereas people that are hypocritical of *Allah*, arrogant to believe the Father now and forever is Jesus, will drop themselves into the dust before the Lord can catch them. As we hope for the best we tend to imagine the worse, regardless we should bring laughter.

Two years at this school, two years of Jesus proving to me that he does exist and losing England was merely the knight moving across the playing field. I failed from King's College London, I didn't even care I was at King's College London, I slightly cared about graduating, but once I asked Jesus to save my life I didn't even care that I failed the third final exam.

My faith fell into Him, nothing mattered anymore. I was surely crazy and now in a land where there was a church on every corner everyone seemed a little crazy. Driving fell away from observing frightened or power tripped individuals to following power lines as they crossed as far as the eye could carry them. My language had also changed, not slightly but dramatically, I spoke in tongue to seniors that could understand and uphold the conversation in this ancient dialect. Not only till much later speaking in tongue was explained to me through reading further passages from Apostle Paul's letters. The Holy Spirit had filled my life.

I was stupid and ran around with idiots who spoke too fast. And the only reason they spoke too fast was as they were scared, no passion but the drive of money. In all sincerity those walking for others should only carry the will of money. Amen. The elderly sample the dirt, and the youth walk around in circles opening the gates of greed wider and not realize the depths of struggles from Russia to Vietnam. If a pagan remains a pagan then we have no room any longer to boast about *Allah*.

"There are six things the Lord hates,
seven that are detestable to Him:
haughty eyes,
a lying tongue,
hands that shed innocent blood,
a heart that devises wicked schemes,
feet that are quick to rush into evil,
a false witness who pours out lies
and a man who stirs up dissension
among brothers."
[Proverbs 6:16-19]

Seventeen

New York wasn't just a place for me to throw up as a child; I attended New York University to sit National American Dental Board Exams, prior to qualifying in England in the hope that I would become a licensed professional in the U.S. as well. I failed two of those four exams and re-sat them in South Carolina, Charleston, where I passed them in December 2004. The phone call was received in a phone booth on a night at the corner of Weston Street, London, finally passed something, great time! Things are moving up in my life.

Just that winter after failing the first final exam attempt I happened to visit the South, met Alicia, one date, a few drinks, her hand into the pocket and a thought of interest to Weston Street Apartments. This ended with an email from her prior to my third examination result, "I'm marrying someone else, sorry." Well that sealed that long distant relationships are tough, never realized they could be pretty short as well. Jesus.

The first arrival to South Carolina was only a few months prior to that, waste of money or need for attention for my father. My sister's sweet sixteenth and a ticket to the S.C. I saw how beautiful the valleys of the South were and was compelled to come back.

My life in England seemed obsolete when I looked out into the morning over the whole of southeast London when I arrived back. Weston Street Apartments for six months with the thought of moving to the States rather than qualifying with a professional degree. Time moved extremely slowly and I was back in the South for summer 2005.

I could hear a little better. The sound of rock music slowly preached worship to my dismay and the sound of listening became apparent, no father, no mother and no sister, only the drive to have another shot. Last shot November 2005, "Jesus, save my life, forgive me for my sins and please help me forgive others." Back to England and back to the South in December 2005.

I lied to my family for weeks before I told them that I actually had failed. I lay on a couch high off my kite whilst I spoke the truth to my mother. The news filtered off my synapses easily. I can only imagine how well they must have thought through their heart at my loss. They happened to handle this pretty well, father and mother worked across the board, across their lives, and worshipped through their beliefs as I battled from east to west. The one that waits with one foot on land and one foot in the sea, amazing to wonder how the story of Christ was so true for me.

That time my strength to speak and work came through a small green leaf and some tobacco, and my faith came through Christ. I returned to England for another six months and back to S.C. in the summer 2006. That was when my father asked some lady what he should do with his son's life.

That angel said: "Start down the one-two-three, S.C. and turn right into Central."

I flew back to England for a week and stamped a visa for five years with the First Wesleyan Church in Central, S.C. Every Sunday from then after I would wake by the sound of a crow cawing on a telephone cross outside my window, I just thanked the Lord. I felt my soul become filled with awareness but with this awareness I had to adjust to the continuous suffering of repentance. Now I pray in the name of Jesus Christ of Nazareth that after being Born Again in His name I am not put to shame. The unusual post was the one written on an altar at the front of the university. A verse written from the book of Isaiah (Old Testament), a verse to fly straight as an eagle, repeated again in the letters of Mark and Luke of the New Testament.

> *"A voice of one calling:*
> *"In the wilderness prepare*
> *the way for the LORD;*
> *make straight in the desert*
> *a highway for our God."*

[Isaiah 40:3]

"The beginning of the good news about Jesus the Messiah, the Son of God, at it is written in Isaiah the prophet:

"I will send my messenger ahead of you, who will prepare your way" – *"a voice of one calling in the wilderness, 'Prepare the way for the Lord, make straight paths for him.'"* [Mark 1:1-3]

> *"A voice of one calling in the desert,*
> *'Prepare the way for the Lord,*
> *Make straight paths for him.*
> *Every valley shall be filled in,*
> *Every mountain and hill made low.*
> *The crooked roads shall become straight,*
> *The rough ways smooth.*
> *And all mankind will see God's*
> *salvation.'"""*

[Luke 3:4-6]

Eighteen

If Job had not have come alive from the Old Testament then he sure did by the new millennium. I suffered plenty, poor little boy from Leicester never really fitting in anywhere or with anyone, not like I really cared what people thought but maybe I should have cared for myself a little. Regardless of the point the Lord had carried me a long way to present me with a new opening. A small university in the middle of farms was celebrating their 100th year of education under Christian theology and a new beginning for someone who barely knew Jesus to understanding that there was someone like him.

The days at Southern Wesleyan University, in Central started slow. Not entirely sure what the reason was for Jesus choosing this school for me or was it just co-incidental? The first person to greet me with a theological emphasis was the daily security man.

He said: "You have the Holy Spirit in you."

With a smile and full devotion to what he said to actually make sense in my tiny receptors of my tiny head. I smiled and thought whatever makes you happy. I felt I was special from my first African brother Godfery from sixth grade had told me with his strong African accent, and now fourteen years later a Southerner twice the age of me was reminding me that Godfery was crazy too.

If that season had not been sanctified within religious writing then I would have no purpose to carry on. The sense of relief that there were some people in the world that thought the same as I was extremely calming. The students needed direction in the twenty-first century and fair-trade for judgment against U.S. soil since 9/11, plus the faculties were old-fashioned and confused on how to preach to a changing generation, that this made the atmosphere all that more electrifying.

The environment changed, everything silenced but crows were heard laughing every time I entered school. There was something scary about crows cawing, as when they are cawing they are not laughing. They are always present in a way that are signalling a time for thought, a time for reflection and a time for appraising the covenant that I made with Lord Jesus Christ. And as the covenant has been made to a superior being I will not hurt my children, there is nothing hygienic about cutting one's self or cutting offspring, the Jews understood the Gospel resurrected. However circumcision was to maintain faith in One God.

Within the first month of a new beginning like any aspect of Job's life I was bound to be tortured. I believed in the Lord and now the evil spirit of God had heard. The Lord is carried across the United States through the law enforcement; unfortunately some officers were more scared of work than the public were of seeing a cop in their rear view mirror. After resisting arrest and a black eye with a scar as a crown I sat down for lunch in the university cafeteria, Al (basketball captain), looked up and laughed. I couldn't help not smile.

Through clearing my name by clearing up Central from trash, and keeping faith and hope Jesus carried me through a year of drug rehabilitation and detoxification whilst attending school and maintaining a positive mental attitude, and the first 100th year of the school's life disappeared faster than the seven years in England.

To be Christian is to be scholarly smart, caring, thoughtful, wise, honourable, considerate, compassionate and offensive in the name of Jesus for enlightening the road to salvation.

Once at SWU, I asked a favour from a student to move herself away from the sight of teaching. She actively was abusing her body to distract the best of us from learning. She racially found that disturbing and made a complaint. Later the Life Support faculties (a country white man and a newly released black slave girl) analyzed that as sexual harassment due to old fashioned ethics and tried to force me out of the school. In chapel I made the men stand and bow for their stupidity that they could not judge for themselves. I was made to forgive the ancient universities corrupt thoughts; personally I hoped for the hypocritical accusers of immorality get struck to the cross with a rusty nail. Hillbilly Christians, who would have thought?

'Everything is meaningless except the fear of the Lord.' Finally sentences written in my language, over and over again came appraisals to learn what *Bhagavan* was trying to teach me. The only observation from my life I could hypothesize is that someone needed me more than my family and all the people in the world needing food. There must have been a reason for filtering my frustration away from Mount Golgotha and to redemption for all eternity.

He was forcing me to repent, I had a lot to repent, I did not wish to repent. Every morning I would wake with my past, I would torture myself with more green drugs that would keep me happy and attentive during classes without resorting to crying over my past. I began to look at things and listen to beings that I would not be a threat.

My wrath maintained itself by the Lord. My disobedient nature to ignorance was lifted, I was no longer afraid of anyone. For Jesus I work and for no one else, for Father I listen and to no one else, and to speak the truth to anyone far from His side was considered pointless.

"Then the LORD said to Cain, "Where is your brother Abel?" "I don't know," he replied. "Am I my brother's keeper?" The LORD said what have you done? Listen! Your brother's blood cries to me from the ground. ... Cain said to the LORD, "My punishment is more than I can bear. ... Then the LORD put a mark on Cain ... This is the written account of Adam's line."

[Genesis 4:9-5:1]

Mornings were at times fogged, bright, cold and rushed. Most people in the United States had cars, most people had trucks and others had bikes. Love God. But what we all had were unethical police and after 9/11 all I could assume was that I did not belong in the States let alone the South.

I drove south on the S.C. 123 and at times in the first year twice over as I needed some form of sedative to pass my day. I travelled further than the number of times Keith Richards played notes on his guitar per minute and all I needed was to eat. Unlike the Apostles I survived eating alone.

What I saw was that most people if not all drove to chase the car in front, most likely a bad habit He says as the car was His to begin with. Best to ease off as in the end we are all going forward, why would one wish to stare at the rear end of my car or your car and not look at the road ahead or the horizon above? In the space of two years from driving between two lanes on a clear road, and undertaking to overtake across three lanes I experienced joy to see that people were beginning to ease; that circling around again to reach a destination was of no dilemma; and that no matter what people drove driving became easier as the lights switched on.

On one of my drives another miracle from above was played for me to endorse when I was being tailed by an erratic driver. I would have normally pulled into a gas station or called someone on the mobile if I was feeling harassed on the road, but once I stopped before a red light and got out my car to engage with the erratic driver. A White man stepped out his car and claimed I had been drinking.

"Do you believe in Jesus?" I said out aloud.

"What's that supposed to mean?" he asked.

"Look at the front of my car," I finished.

Not only had I two dents on my bonnet, one accidental and one purposeful for symmetry, but also my front license plate read, 'Southern Wesleyan University.'

"Oh my God," he said, and we departed.

The days change in the South from cold quiet mornings, to warmer afternoons, to even warmer afternoons, to warm evenings, to cool nights. For me they mixed as one, the one covered in a cloud of smoke and false sense of euphoria. I began watching the shadows inside trees, and following telephone lines whilst driving, hawks, buzzards, crows, robins, common grackles, American Kestrels, cows and horses all tried to catch my attention but the only attention I began to pay was in God.

Still total darkness, I searched for caves and my search resulted into anything black, a television frame, a pen, a stereo speaker, just beneath the horizon, until I wished to picture black with my eyes open. I thank the Lord again to have given me strength and the will to fight against oppression from comfortably fed communities. The Lord has served His people well, however the people have a hard time serving their fellow men and segregation still existed.

Red: When everything is off than nothing would be on, thus something has to always remain on for it to be off, right? What's the puzzle is when One decides to switch off, (how do you have a conscious my Lord?), then heaven shall be closed also. Neither for the One or heaven shall this happen, as throughout all of space was given a place where life was allowed to bloom, and Heaven dwells to return back to the One.

People had difficulty speaking out aloud, like there was some curse, possibly the curse was me. As I walked with a smile in my brain and black for my sight I noticed that there were others around me, and with others our expectations for life climbed. The cry of the old and the weak became more apparent and the cause for righteousness built. Some preachers and tutors at the school spoke words of confidence and reassurance that I had never been accustomed to hear before. Chapel services began with the need to hear these words of truth, hope and faith. Jesus began to enrich my soul with the stamp that my life was only worth living for him and his Father.

Nineteen

Time was not only spent with my books as I made a new life in the country, even though there is nothing wrong with spending time with books. I had a little more responsibility on my plate. Father and mother had invested into a gas station, and all their time was spent managing the open all around the clock service policy to reduce costs. Before my actual stay I aided assistance and most of the times the assistance was appreciated, however after my final failure and division into the new school I resorted into a state of darkness. My duties to my work were no longer on the cards and watching my parents singularly handle the third world of the New World began my teaching in the people of the covenant.

Jesus Christ was not playing around when he waited for time to dissolve my life, and He would have waited on the telephone star outside the gas station for me to ask for salvation. He taught me at school the principle of the Testaments and as soon as possible to the gas station to watch how worshippers of all groups worked with one another. I had no life except the one to lead in St. George's footsteps, no one to believe anymore than the theology of masoretes, and letters from apostles and gospels and, stories listing prophecies that the communities of people driving into the gas station were more familiar with than I.

Sales is a difficult business especially if you were wearing my shoes; on one hand I have to maintain a positive mental attitude with the customer and the other with my family. British English on a brown person was heard as a pleasant surprise to most customers but to my parents an utter disappointment. The grammar and the vocabulary were from the devil's lips and absolutely no sentence could be interpreted as humor when the eyes of the evil spirit of God dwelled in me.

The first couple of months to winter 2006 were spent by smoking heavily on the way to work at the gas station from school. One life changes and another begins like some performer changing clothes between takes. I was too soaked in narcotics to make any difference except that of keeping pleasantries during business hours. Father did not make things any easier, he'll wait to catch me with a cigarette and impound his power of authority and make the day much warmer than a normal day in peachy South.

I met many people placing Christ words at my lips, most were well organized citizens, and even more were working folk of Christ with names as David, Christopher, Matt, John, Joshua, Justin and Deborah. They viewed me as whatever they thought and I viewed them through the words of the Holy Bible.

People worship in the South if not only on Sundays then on Wednesday evenings as well. There is much similarity in the belief of the cross; however I felt that no matter how hard I tried to preach the word of God being true nobody would look after the precious land unless they were awarded with money or an awareness week.

The letter of Corinthians and the book of Isaiah reflected my image on how to forgive the people towards their repulsion from one another. Black people mostly believed they were still segregated from the rest of the world as Nadine Gordimer would illustrate through her story "As Others See Us." And the Whites needed reminding that they still should believe in the one Spirit.

As I was of British culture I heard remarks of envy and pessimism, asking reassurance of Christ's love amongst themselves either by labels as black or red necked. Mind you I had no problem with the Confederacy but most Blacks would involve me into their world of sin due to the slavery encountered half a century ago. Personally they probably wished to speak freely and as I had no problem speaking to the ones that turned White, along without any form of religious fundamentalism, I spoke to the blacks as well.

Most days I would have worked without saying a word. I smiled graciously and looked at the display on the register feeling more baffled about living here than the customers who had lived here ever did. And for all I began to question the Lord further.

Gracias Dios for *Mexicanos*. They made my day circulate; end of the day and *amigos* together would come to buy beer. Laughing and joking amongst themselves brought a little more stubble to my day.

Mostly the day went by spending time to manage the gas station and watching a bird perched on a telephone line stretching across the S.C. 153. I watched him and he watched whatever pleased his fancy. We then watched for familiar customers that enjoyed having a laugh, most familiars who enjoyed being a comedian. Chris, Justin, Cedrick, Patsy are just a few who believed in nothing besides keeping a good sense of humour. The days got warmer and standing behind a glass window facing west the shifts turned to help me sleep.

My father flew to India in winter of 2006 as my grandfather died. He spent three months in

India and my mother, sister and I managed the store. There was another lady who worked hard and she worked through suffering attacks of pneumonia, the lady believed in Christ and her husband and children are good. The lovely sufferer suffered further as I threw her pocketbook across the room once as I was searching for something to hit a thief with. The thief drove away and I happened to had broken her phone. I'm sorry.

Thank God my spirit had been filled and that grace follows tremendous disappointment. Thank Jesus for the hypnotizing *kama* of the traffic that flowed by the gas station. Staring right through the traffic unwound my nerves from the past seven years. Work at the gas station flew from days to nights, and pleasant evenings with gentle conversations with officers to young girls that they hired to buy alcohol. Times at the gas station were a blast, a time to reflect and heave balance into my life, and appreciate life.

I turned floats and studied at the same time. Marijuana helped strongly on most days, especially those where work had to be done. By summer of 2007 most was about to change. A year into moving and becoming accustomed to American law, Americans and my family I entered another part of Greenville's best.

After clearing all PTI criteria I forced myself into a drug rehabilitation centre. I spent three months entering trials on why drugs were bad and finding my route out. The summer heat was intense. I spent most of the summer earning credentials in physics and psychology at Greenville Tech. Placing all my homework in one sitting and saving pennies so I could pay for rehabilitation classes, and then to the gas station so my poor old man could take a break from working around the clock spent most my time.

Whilst I sat solving my new life at Greenville Tech registration I watched the news, the act of arson towards Virginia Tech College, mass killings by a stupid individual that ended by him taking his own life. One way or another but not both, what's the point of killing others beside himself alone? He deserves for no reincarnation.

The news showed other shootings at schools and this being the worst. Now I'm in America and there is plenty of room for improvement, some people are not religious as they are afraid, or have they suffered intense pressure from the law or community that they wish for no youth to suffer the same, or …

I remember one day a Christ believer declined me from looking at her notes. Worst still she filled her pride by lending the notes to someone else. In frustration I wanted to key her car for falsely portraying in Christ. An act of God was shown to me on that day. Whilst waiting to release my anger a dozen crows stepped into sight on the roof ledge of Ruth A. Nicholson Building, at

Greenville Tech, and began watching me to make my next move. The Father was close; I calmed myself, stepped into my car and drove to work.

Maxim, Time, The Greenville News, USA Today, "A packet of Marlboro Light," says a customer, back to work, and math, and Scripture, and staring at a distant cross, singing to music, finding the scores for Clemson Tigers, reading a little more Scripture, tapping my fingers to a beat, "Cash these in and give me another 20," back to Scripture and time to adjust to my love is true.

There were times when differences came to view; quick judgmental men who came to force a fight as I shouted to stop their child running across the parking ground. Luckily the man was still a father as my shout made a car stop before the child. Be cautious men of allowing spoilt women to look after your sons when they flock together, instead of taking care of the young they tend to take care of themselves. Then there was a woman who was envious and loud as she knows best because she came from Brooklyn, and a dude from Washington D.C. that I asked if he was gay, a simple no would have been fine.

Across nights most if not all shop doors were closed regardless if they were open for service or not. During Christmas night 2006, roughly around two in the morning I sat facing the wall inside the gas station. A car pulled into the bay outside and to the entrance came two young men. One pushed hard on the door to enter and to his surprise the door swung open, he looked at me, I turned my head to look at him. His faith made him react and through his alarm he went back to the car and put something away. He came back with his wallet.

The importance of the day still plays heavy on my mind, as an hour after the boys had left they arrived again with their mother. A woman who seemed to be heavy on crack, the clothes she wore did not seem to fit her and she came in asking her children to rob me. That night I spoke only to the children and they listened, that night I saw that no matter how hard her children would pray for their mother, she would have to learn to pray for herself.

"It gave me great joy when some believers came and testified about your faithfulness to the truth, telling how you continue to walk in it. I have no greater joy than to hear that my children are walking in the truth. Dear friend, you are faithful in what you are doing for the brothers and sisters, even though they are strangers to you."

[3John 1:3-5]

Completely off the scales some people choose to live in the United States, and disturbing to hear how they are kept on living by society. One Saturday afternoon I saw an ugly evil world. A woman who spent time in the store alone and then got argumentative as she had not filled her own lottery numbers right. Just then a man walks in and flashes a police badge declaring that he was a cop from Philadelphia and could 'make things worse.' Something he must have heard in a movie. Now how many stores had these fools harassed? I spoke, he stared, and he left and for me to pray for him makes no sense. The way I interpreted his behaviour from my classes that summer was that he was filled with the evil in the Bible and no Jesus to set him free. Instead he shadowed behind a Jezebel making trouble to boast his ego to hell.

Cannot finish with a frown, the old man that has worked all day on the railroads is about to buy his beer and me thinking through Jesus will not be acceptable, a little sugar, and a little sitting and staring at the distant nail on the cross. There he comes pulling into Raceway Gas Station on S.C. 153 from Exit 40 off the I-85 in his 01 orange Dodge Charger with flag and horn.

"How's it going?" said the old man.

Twenty

So who's to say that we should follow religion and not Darwin's theory of evolution and natural selection, that man came from apes and no creativity falls on theology? Thus we are more like monkeys than meets the eye.

Two monkeys were sitting on a branch arguing over who will eat the last mango, squawking and shaking the branch they were sitting on and snap goes the branch. Both monkeys fall on the ground ass first and stare up at the sky when a shooting star crosses the night space. One monkey looks at the other and the other says "God" with a long pause, and events as such through time got called and God became a necessity for the monkeys to share. Then the monkey bought a coat and a hat and so did the other, and so they all copied one from another to get to understand God better. But did humans come from monkeys? Who cares? I say where did the monkeys come from?

Overall the Lord made everything, but He made humans that more special, or maybe the humans made the Lord from all the children suffering from slavery in the time of first human civilization. Who knows? And now really who cares? As long as there is a Lord, an *Allah*, a *Bhagavan* and monkeys sitting on branches then we are all fine.

Tender loving care was now needed for most monkeys that have bared a burden. As for my parents there are many wonderful points about them. They fed, bathed, and dressed me. They are passionate about what they do and beginning to understand what I do. They passed a bipolar condition to me but after treatment I realised that some monkeys are just best to let be.

"You know that when you were pagans, somehow or other you were influenced and led astray to mute idols. Therefore ... know that no one who is speaking by the Spirit of God says, "Jesus be cursed," and no one can say, "Jesus is Lord," except by the Holy Spirit."

[1Corinthians 12:2-3]

Narcotics were still pretty much in my life even though I had moved country and sold my life to Jesus Christ. Initially I just needed something to relax with, something to concentrate on, and something to help me not to repent, and to stay head strong on where I am and what I had to do. Marijuana kept me straight. I was able to attend S.W.U. and live life with my family as long as I had a ready supply of anti-depressants then I handled all work and attitudes thrown at me well.

After I had been arrested at Greenville I almost lost my angle and began taking cocaine again. The last time I had done that drug was in England and now I took one hit and felt great. Throughout the first season in the United States after university and at times during university I would have taken a hit and sit in class or at a friends recuperating from the effect on preventing repentance. Mostly I didn't care as long as I passed my day alive I would try again the next day to cycle a better road to salvation. The year of 2006 ended and so did my ridiculous need for powder. I started gargling and spitting remnants out my nostrils with water. With every spit I felt liberated.

Nevertheless marijuana still stayed in my life, well until the days after my graduation from Southern Wesleyan. By now I needed a comfortably rolled joint mostly everyday to and from school. Sometimes I would feel so terrible in the mornings that the first thing to satisfy my necessity to live was to pull over at the closest gas station and have the smoke.

Regardless of all the cruelness printed in the media and in legal circles marijuana ended up taking my life but I needed it for a new one. Never smoke alone, and only smoke around the right crowds, on vacation, over thirty and possibly tax as the effect to solidify normal physiological systems with a drug that causes hallucinogenic effects can be devastating on the ignorant mind. Thanks to my Lord He has shown me that everything comes in moderation and like alcoholism; drug use is most harmful when taken alone.

Unlike England I smoked this time to love Jesus. Jesus knows what is wrong and I smoking was definitely one of them. My road was paved for forgiving and this has helped me reach realization after being lost in my wilderness for so long. I smoked so much that I figured out that hydrogen chloride in eye drops vasoconstricts the blood capillaries from our eyes enough for the passage of THC in marijuana to be filtered straight to the kidneys. Hence reducing the effects of marijuana to the brain and helping me regain full consciousness at a greater rate. The oxymoron description illustrates that smoke on one hand and wash on the other makes no sense. And slowly I began to understand the need to stop.

How would I be able to help others when I am not at my best? Jesus helped me when I was not at my best and now I should prove to him that I could help him further than the communities that remembered Him ever did. And help the communities that have been greeted by wealth and forgotten that love could exist. Love is to ask a question without the intention of receiving an answer that is love. Love is to chill.

Thank God that I was able to maintain cool around these new people. The New World can be pretty old fashioned. I am here to try and walk in the path of a man named Jesus, a book of Isaiah and a flock of sheep, mostly black and white sheep but some brown sheep too or another sheep following a shepherd.

Climbing out of the hole and into a new life whilst maintaining a positive English attitude that all English share when not at home; smile at outlaws and sheriffs, check for pulse and breathing, and instead of calling the police call a paramedic for emergencies.

From coming into awareness I found the strength in pray. I would usually sit with my hands together in pray whilst watching television. For a lengthy amount of time I would just sit and watch my hands, through my hands, at the horizons that my fingers would give. Several months of doing this my hands began to move. I used my fingers to tap against each other to bring momentum back into my life. Much later the tapping of fingers became mapping of ideas. I learnt how to move my hands to revise structure and remember vast quantities of information in a short amount of time.

I called moving my hands through and over each other, 'mapping', where the rest came from them being together. Lord Jesus helped me to build strength by pushing my hands together at times, and with this my muscles came alive to the tips of my toes. As long as my hands were together I was fine and as long as I did not have to scroll them to warn others off they were also fine.

I learned that two emotions that exist in the world but we live to try to hide them are experiencing humiliation and embarrassment. People acted in horrible ways to me to save themselves from these emotions. So now I do not feel humiliation or embarrassment. I confessed my sins to Lord Jesus Christ. The answer to overcome humiliation and embarrassment was water, 'Holy Water,' drink and have strength to forgive and forget. Night will come and day will follow. My actions by smoking scratched me, but that scratch adapted me to drink water in presenting situations.

Lord make me well and help me grow, help me help others grow so we can show love for you, however if I still fumble please allow me to remember your good name, and help me show others that salvation is only through you. Amen, Matthew, sounds as thank you.

Twenty One

The clock was ticking and the ladies of S.W.U. are about to make a close win, with ball in hand the shot is taken in the final seconds of second half. Clang bounces the ball to the opposition and the final whistle blows. The score is tied and I walk out of the arena. Instead of sitting and supporting a good cause at the Lord's graveyard I decided to get up and leave as I had an important test on folklore, and I had no idea what that meant.

The class had a teacher who smiled and enforced a positive but rather superficial teaching environment. She was all smiles and nerves; I would have been the same if I met an Israeli worshipping Indian. Questions were way past her ability to answer, and she had failed not only to provide me with a good definition of folklore, but also limited the amount of questions I could ask in the classroom. Thanks to the literature necessary for class I found what folklore meant to me. Unfortunately this was after that test, but to me folklore could easily be defined as *Ramayan* or *Mahabharath*. She spoke about urban legends and whatever; probably if she gave herself credit for the amount she knew or full sincerity and courage in believing in Christ she would have been able to understand that I still didn't understand, and wished I did. Fired!

The men nights in basketball were pumped for both home and opposition. The passion towards the end of the season was one to be admired; every athlete was also a mercenary. I presented myself in a crowd for Christian vowed basketball players to bring the atmosphere alive. Times became violent when the times exceeded levels of tears but they were also there to remember.

A beautiful moment to consider the path of faith; I was standing next to the bleaches where friend, Daryll, top scorer on board and ball, was watching me throw hoops during half time at one of our games. With ball in hand I looked off his horizon and then at him, then I looked at the net, saw Daryll and threw once, missing the rim and net. Time slowed and collecting the ball I made my way to space again on left wing outside the three. Daryll waited for me to notice him, and noticing him I stood, we smiled at each other and I released the ball. Still seeing Daryll the net swishes, he stood up, and stepped off the bleaches over my right shoulder, and a ball got thrown to him. Three, after three, after three rained aim to our faith from Daryll hands.

S.W.U. had a good atmosphere; from a guy on crutches, to a girl in a wheelchair, to another girl that was paraplegic, to a one armed man, to me, Shankar, to all the fallen leaves on the road there the times were unbelievable. There were chapel services organized by the students and very well talented teachers twice a week as a part of the curriculum.

My time sitting in chapel started with pure silence. Everyone was listening to the speaker and I was thinking of this Lord, and finding a safe spot to stare at and provide the speaker a safe blinking distance to speak. I stared at anything that was black, the light would have obviously hurt and I could see through blackness. Further past the pitcher the better to maintain focus on the delivery as well as devotion in the one Spirit. I could see everything that I left behind; I could see the mercy that a poor person has to face. Two years went from staring at anything that was black, preferably what was linear in my visual field, to picturing black, to bowing and watching my hands and feet pay respect for the speaker's life as well as my own.

Nothing moves when you look down, well except for Earth, and a fly that appears from the light and searches for a dark spot to wait for the light again. Instead he finds me searching for what he has mercy to fly and find. And both of us sit and wait with our mouths open waiting for the other to feast on. Time ticks by and chapel service closes with "Amen." Times in chapel moved from finding me to finding out where I was.

The people around me were not at all like the people on the road that brought me to Southern Wesleyan. The smiles, appraisals, Davey, mulch, Jessica, song sparrows, the gym floor, Duncan, rock, Craig, Brandon, Java, Rickman, Tom, John, more mulch, Joe, the ladybirds, planting flowers, the Maintenance Crew, and Stefanie brought my understanding that Carolina Chickadees too wait. Love God.

Around campus was beautiful. The university sat on a hill previously known as Cottage Hill and all corners of the sky could be seen. The east had the best view; every morning I would park the car mostly to see the sunrise and the crows watching the sunrise too. The atmosphere was firstly quiet. A confused individual faced the walls of religion and mentoring that no one should be trusted but Jesus. I kept my walk alive in Jesus surprised that He could bring me to such a secluded space in the universe to teach me that He is alive.

I was twenty-six entering a hundred year anniversary of this school. The Lord exists was carved onto a statue of a Red-Indian warrior holding an eagle at the end of Wesleyan Drive with a quote from the book of Isaiah. There was a statue of a bronze Jesus praying whilst bronze children read and played around Him. (Please Lord make my brother well).

By the end of two years I had not only become educated in science but also in religion, history, aesthetics, performing arts, landscaping, mechanics and physics. I still had no idea what I was doing there, everyone seemed much better willed without a spoilt, stupid, Jesus walker ruining the mentality of his or her own world.

Through the long winding roads from Central S.C. to home or the gas station times were absolutely silent in my head. On the drives I listened to music and did as much as possible to prevent me from repenting. Unfortunately I tried not to repent. In my mind I hummed *Om* to fill the silences and cover the sounds of frustration. I later realized *Ommm...* in the mind helped me listen. (I learnt this whilst reading over noise in the library). I give all that I can to the survival of the Lord Jesus Christ, Christ Jesus, and Jesus Christ again except for the small print, repent. I miss sports with my mates.

Believing in the Father was a birthright and a curse for me, and only became faith when I read the Bible to be true. The way I thought was right but the way I read was extremely different. I had no idea that reading in this form would not only save my life but would help one another to save each other. We may not speak the same language and a curse on reticules may prevent bonding but the deliver to The Creator exists. And as our gift for being human we should make a choice to follow Him put the Earth through the eye of a needle and fight into shadows or not.

Once on my mornings to school suffering from repentance and confusion of anger in forgiving Jesus Christ too, and all his people that surrounded my life at this time I stopped on the road. The road lifted to the horizon and all I saw were red lights and an idiot tailing onto my rear. I hate that, all the road in the world behind us and especially behind him but he decides to give me a push up the hill. I stopped then began slowly climbing the hill whilst watching him come to a complete stop and climbing again. He was the coach of the team. I had no idea and felt a little uneasy around him. I can understand now how Jesus being a Saviour to all forgiveness's can be hurt when asked for forgiveness again.

The baseball lads at Southern Wesleyan were incredible. I don't know who loved them more, the girls or me. They all had a different testimony and all were suffering from some form of spiritual breakage of bread, along with winter season to summer season and over again they will be remembered forever. (Overall the strategy is simple: enjoy university, don't think about rushing it, not even to please the ones you love and enjoy university). The seasons ended for glory and eternal love with the construction of a new chapel.

The Lord's Pray

"Our Father in heaven,
hallowed be thy name,
your kingdom come,
your will be done,
on earth as it is in heaven.
Give us today our daily bread.
And forgive us our debts,
as we also have forgiven our debtors.
And lead us not into temptation,
but deliver us from the evil one
For yours is the kingdom,
and the power and the glory forever.
Amen."

[Matthew 6:9-13 (KJV)]

Twenty Two

Smoking is over. I discovered stamina fat burners, took one, and my taste for food returned and the dismissal for all smoking became extinguished. I cannot believe my PTI advisor clinically signed me for drug rehabilitation like some awful shrink and did not consider advising a little caffeine instead. For some this may not work because they may have a low body mass index in comparison to the carbohydrate intake needed to manage fat burners, or are suffering extreme depression.

However a sincere 'I'm sorry for you smoking' from my parents at sixteen would have worked just as well.

Then again I think that in the long run the tree of life could become legalized. Place the middleman into a factory that buys at wholesale, and prices a tax to ages over twenty-five or thirty.

The family labourer has realized some form of comfort to his found life, his sense of comfort is resolved and mine too, as fear of crime from ugly cops and weak providers of cannabis would burn out. A packet of ten sticks of marijuana at a reasonable price, the farmers happy and there are more honest jobs for the middle men making me happy. Above all keeping strict guard on age of consumers would need to be a must.

Now that was how I learnt all cookies crumble, how the sunsets and how the Lord may have had nothing to do with my life. I have potential for skill and heard tribute from Charlie that the Holy Spirit is within me. So can I give something that thousands believe to be love on credit? All my mistakes have foiled into meaning and this is my fault too. What I see through my eyes gazing into a mirror is not what I wish to see, instead I want to see how it would have been if I was the Holy Spirit at twelve. The only way to know the Lord is to feel and show love around the clock, with credit. Help someone stand or call a paramedic instead of the sheriff when guiding the sinners to a wall and pushing their face into it. Learn to read what has been written as words. The Lord had everything to do with it.

We do what we do to better the future that we can make. We don't do what we do for ourselves as we find enrichment by paying thanks to what we are given. Those that don't follow by us will feel the raft of our dwelled anger in this lifetime let alone the next. A stone to be thrown by my right arm flew across S.C. 153, to smash the rear window of a thief stealing sixty dollars of gasoline. The oil-rig then followed to replace my stolen gasoline crushing the thief metaphorically under its mighty wheels. And so the wheel that keeps spinning us can collect souls to keep spinning wheels to bring us closer to enlightenment.

Patiently waiting for papers to be signed and approved by seniors that passion for soul inspiration can be delivered to others and now I wait. Waiting can be tough, stare at a wall or just between the faces to notice the vase falling and making a sound. Interesting really to read in between the lines, then again there is nothing more significantly pleasing than observing or harnessing Absolute Truth.

Three Absolute Truths besides the fact that we all live together; explaining these to adolescence will make everyone's life sound: The sense of sight, the sense of sound and the sense of strength. (Those accumulating money will be oblivious and reluctant of using these until inevitable suffering comes to hand. Better to be prepared for salvation than to hope for adaptation).

The sense of sight means finding fixed points in an environment, anything black is the greatest used fixed point to find standing in a changing environment. Muslims have the Black Stone, Hindus have the black *Shivlinga* and Christians have the tomb where Jesus rested. Through the darkness we wait to be enlightened by the Lord and should be placed before you and I. Horizons off people, off objects, and between the land and the sky are the best sources for thought.

With realisation of colour we also have red and light. Red symbolises love and affection, we are red. And the light, the light gives us power, light is everything that cannot be black or red. All three colours working in harmony are monopoly.

The sense of sound comes from the sound of *Om*. (ॐ) The 'o' makes the inhale for a long exhale '*mmm…*' Used for peace and used for awareness, and concentration to surrounding sound, speech and music, the sound of peace is voiced subliminally. The opposite would be a screech.

The sense of touch means to place one's fingertips and thumbs together. This is to bring about neural stability, to stable the pulse of the heartbeat and with force will increase human strength. Those with one arm should place the first and next finger with thumb together. Then again those with two arms could use this method also.

When no bread or wines are close then this Absolute Truth can be found. When these truths are practiced there is only one outcome. When sitting, watching, listening to the only time given the inevitable outcome would be to let go and fall asleep. On the contrary a large glass of water would stimulate the senses to rest, exhibiting one to awake. From peace there comes life so reflect these to those that are clearly in need. And as I was made to suffer to bless you with spiritual fullness you will be blessed when sharing Absolute Truth wholeheartedly.

On the whole I wait to yawn into a mirror, I also wish I was a little bit shorter, much sober and much further than any sand trap that I can make a prison from to live or dissolve in. Unfortunately I spelt out a life that was supposed to bring fortune and glory to all but instead brought me closer to suffer. Fine to the ravens, and fine to the beasts, fine to all the creatures with more than four legs plus fine to making things extinct.

"Fear the LORD your God, serve him only and take your oaths in his name. Do not follow other gods, the gods of the peoples around you; for the LORD your God, who is among you, is a jealous God and his anger will burn against you, and he will destroy you from the face of the land."
[Deuteronomy 6:13-15]

Make something to live in with wood and iron to reach one light year per sec and let us call that day Universal Day. Plan to blow up any trespasser to our land with a nuke at night for the prime purpose of wellness of others need to repent.

Galaxies before the cosmos all must wait before the Lord as I too be fully delivered from all my sin, and bring one child to understand how to live through retribution. Twitch the toes to show the young their need to wait in respect. And they too shall surely come before the God of all that flies with precision.

Flies fly with precision, and as much as it amazes me to watch that they too do not fly straight into the light now but into the darkness waiting for light to shine their life, just as I stare beneath the horizon and wait.

Working, labour and volunteer, reading and writing, assuming that my refundable Playstation works to have a slow contest with Spiderman fighting the Masters of Evil from consuming the planet. Then pass further time eating, shitting and reading the funnies from the antique black and white. This is what I pray for. This, and working, building, reading, helping, waiting and watching with my eyes closed or watching through a wall, waiting. Waiting patiently when all absolutes of my life become short enough to reach infinity. *Dichosos los Dios* that prison is more peaceful for me than suicide now. Crazily blessed is the way I which to live.

So let us wait like crows for the occasion and you will wait patiently for the arrival to the land far from any brick wall and stoned ground. Until then I will smile, and pay for some dentures and share laughs without speaking around Wesleyan throughout time. Is that you Ryan? One press up, two press ups, three press ups, four. One elephant, two elephants, three elephants, four elephants and more. An apple for me and an apple for you mate! Now I pray to pay scientists and watch them build De Loreans that can pull me to the opposite ends of space. *Om Shanti* to me and *Om Shanti* to you, and embrace me with love that I lost for others.

Thank God I know now to bow longer so my *Allah* does not. As if there's no one watching over me then there's no one watching over you. And I've been travelling unwillingly since smashing a mirror deliberately that resulted with seven years painfully disappearing faster than Hiroshima, Lord. I've begun to eat cattle as they are holy. How somebody heard the last grain of sand in a sandglass disintegrate still amazes me. But then again so does a Harley's roar, a crow's caw, a baby beginning to laugh, a woman cheering, a helicopter whirring, a child making a touchdown, a man dwelling, and leaves rustling and yet I still hear vast suffering. I might as well not have heard anything, no rustling leaves, no babies laughing, no people dancing, no shines of moonlight over midnight waves, no turtledoves, no rum in my throat, no hammers on fire bells, no rain falling, no elephants marching and no ten men to one man singing to mow or their dog. GRRR!

EPILOGUE

I hope to have encouraged all people to live life in a means for peace. For today's world compared to that of the Romans there is so much to do. Some would say that the twenty-first generation populations have times much difficult than our fathers before us. As there are more distractions there are more possible ways to sin. However let us keep our minds to the future as too the children that we grow surely have to die. Let us build faith on love so they can have reason behind their need to repent. For no reason should I have moved, I should have waited and worked well for my future investments.

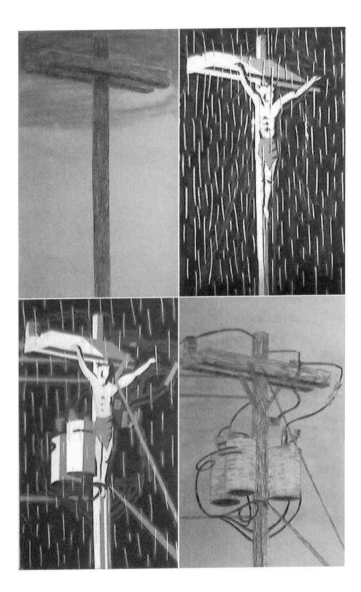

Short Spirit Stories

These short stories are life occurrences that have remained as significant memories in which Shankar had developed his spirit to the Word of God.

Before A.D.

A Hindu lad asked a Muslim lass out on a date in the corridor outside their chemistry class. Muslim lass was not with a hijab in those days at Queen Elizabeth I College. The sixteen year olds were fond of each other. The lad as the lass was attractive and the lass as the lad was smart and popular I guess. She said she'd think about the date so not to damage the lad's confidence.

Hindu lad was walking to the canteen with Vassell and another friend when a Muslim lad shoulder barged him from behind walking ahead. As the Hindu lad asked what was that for? The Muslim threatened the Hindu amongst their peers.

"You asked out Amina, didn't you? Why did you ask her? Don't you know she's my girl?" informed Omar, the Muslim lad.

"I had no idea she was anyone's," Shankar, the Hindu lad replied.

"She is single, but she is still my girl. You think you're so smart. Meet me after college in Victoria Park. You're dead!" said Omar.

He then walked down the corridor with his Muslim lads pleased at what he said leaving Shankar trembling in his boots. Trying to keep composure amongst his friends he carried on the walk to the canteen.

The news travelled fast amongst the Hindu's and the Muslim's until it reached the ears of a Sikh. Gurpreet, I think was his name. He approached Shankar with a laugh and a smile.

"I hear you have to fight Omar over a girl," said Gurpreet. "Don't go to the park, go straight home. I will see to Omar, and just come to college as normal tomorrow and everything will be settled. And stay away from Amina."

Hindu lad did what Sikh lad said. Quietly and quickly he walked through Victoria Park to the bus stop and back home. Arrived back to college the next day and the news arrived from Vassell during a morning smoke beside the wall to the door into the building.

"They met yesterday. Gurpreet said he had told you to go home and to leave you alone or he'd have him and his crew to deal with," said Vassell.

And that was that. Shankar saw Omar around the college and slowly ignoring lead to hello's as Omar asked, and made a relationship with Amina. Amina began to wear a hijab and still kept smiles with Shankar. Nothing more happened after that between the Hindu lad and the Muslims.

A booming college life commenced from sixteen to eighteen. Shankar never fully understood what had happened and what could have happened, so I'll stay with the facts. He was the most popular Hindu lad at college due to his charisma and respect from others he received. He was possibly the smartest, with everyone knowing the richest due to his father.

Anyone who lived in the area of Evington knew of Shankar's father by name through their parent's. His father's employees were mostly Indian, Hindu's and Sikh's with an occasionally Muslim coming in and out of the family business of garment manufacturing. Anyone who was anyone knew the name, 'Roma Knitwear Ltd', was owned and managed by four brothers, with the eldest brother being Shankar's father. Henceforth don't wake up the Hindu lad after his father has tried hard to keep him sleeping. Who knows why he did that? But don't wake up Shankar, as the motivation and innocent behavior of Shankar may change; and the Sikh's and Muslim's would be placed in their place as the Hindu takes his.

Good grades across the board not for just the Hindu lad but for many of the students at Q.E. Hindu lad was asked out by soon after by Aliya, another Muslim lass, as she liked him for his smarts. They dated for a season.

Years ahead as the Hindu lad was failing his degree taking reflection in Bradford with Vassell, smoking heavy ganja still asleep in all regards to the spirit, Omar walked into the house. Omar was married to Amina whilst studying for a degree together. No fear felt just friendship. *Masha'Allah.*

"The horse is made ready for the day of battle, but victory rests with the Lord."　　　[Proverbs 21:31]

"Rich and poor have this in common: The Lord is the Maker of them all."　　　[Proverbs 22:2]

The day had turned into night. The night was during the cold season and I was with Romeo ordering ourselves a lamb donor with chips from the most famous take-away restaurant, Chickin-Lickin, on Melton Road, Leicester. Romeo as always was willing to help 'probably' just to see me make a fool of myself or appease me due to my bad attitude. That night did happen to become one.

Before I commence this quick moment in time that would finish in the blink of an eye for me the depth of the crack in time would continue forever even after receiving forgiveness.

I was asking for this, I was feeling uneasy; I was in the mode of self-sabotage. I had no praises on holding myself together and no respect prior to what was to happen and definitely there would be no respect thereafter. Who I wanted the respect, value, regards, warm love from was my mother and my father, but as they were only concerned with words associated with my degree in dentistry what was happening with my emotions was going a miss. So self-sabotage and move on, live and experience a better university life was on my mind, but how to break this to Lara was the question.

I stepped out my BFF's car around the corner to Lara's house. I can't remember if I called her or threw tiny stones to her window for her to let me in. She opened her door like she did many times before this one whilst her parents and brother were already in bed. I was wearing heavy tracksuit bottoms that with every step up the steps the fabric brushed together making noise. What was I thinking? What a fool I was with the sound and with the smell of the donor with chips late in darkness to a quiet sleeping house which wasn't even mine I was obviously going to be caught.

Up the stairs and into Lara's room. She had her light on and I immediately just sat on the side of her bed to dig into my meat and potatoes. There was a knock on her door. I saw her eyes dilate and my heart skipped a beat.

"Who's there?" she asked.

Her mother knew of our relation but not us actually being together in their home for the night. (Not as this was the first night, but it was the last).

181

Lara's dad replied, "What's that smell? Are you okay? Let me in."

There was nowhere to hide. I thought to hide under the covers behind the bed, but there was no hiding the smell of the food. And before I could react to hide her father pushed open the door that she had slightly opened to speak with him.

With me being as tall as him, the light in the room extinguished as two bodies, plus Lara's mother, including Lara stood together. I didn't know what to say. I also wanted out of the relationship but not secure to lay the cards on the table. Her dad went to slap me but I dodged the hit. This is where I should have become a man and explained to him, or at least apologized. I thought for many years to have everyone move to the lounge, apologize for meeting as such, and declare my love for Lara. Instead I stepped forward for him to have another go to slap me. He did. Without a word I walked downstairs and out of her house.

Lara made an excuse that I had nowhere to stay as my parents were out of town and taken the keys to my house. I called Romeo to come and pick me up and so to stay at his instead. Before we returned to his, through my frustrations I threw the food away and he gave a small laugh.

Even after the whole situation I still didn't act quite like a man. She was hurt, she was hurting, and she was hurt more when I spent time with my friends instead of coming to a solution with her. I also for no reason was awful to her younger brother as he was at times my bridge to getting to her. Also with cannabis and friends that smoked drugs, they all played together to have the best of me.

So to place icing on the cake of break-ups was of no surprise. There was a Muslim guy that liked Lara very much and in those days I had no say to women let alone to a Muslim brother. She spoke to him, and he was thus in awe for her, which I don't blame him in the slightest. One fine day outside Romeo's sitting in Mike's car with Romeo and Vassell at the back, Lara's hit-man had seen me. He pulled up by the car I was in and with his friend ordered me to get out but I didn't. I did want to, I guess I could have, but this was a fight I didn't want to win. This was a hit that I thought I deserved, and facts would say I did. Whilst my friends just sat in the car, Lara's hit-man and his friend laid into me through the passenger window. The whole incident was obviously a football injury when it came to explaining to my parents why I had a black-eye. Mother did ask once long after what had happened about Lara. Well, 'Lara and I have moved on,' what else?

"Stay away from the foolish man, for you will not find knowledge on his lips"

[Proverbs 14:7]

Stage Hotel, Leicester, that's where literally the stage was set for my 21st birthday party. Friends of course, extended friends and their families, my family of course and my extended family and friends of family too. For me it was my 21st birthday and for my father it was a chance to show what he and his money can do. The food was of course free, but also were the drinks at the bar which I did ask my father not to put forward, but my father was my father and like me he liked to without thinking twice make others happy.

A day before the big day I met up with friends to have a private night out with just them. Having heavy smokes of green herb by the canal that flowed by De Montfort University is where the night began. I was with Romeo, Vassell, Mike, and Vassell's female friend. Smokes finished so we headed under the bridge to the bar above. BANG!

"Hahahahaha!" Mike laughed.

In conversation with Vassell's friend I accidently had hit the iron bar under the bridge with my forehead. It was a heavy hit. My big forehead vibrated an echo under the whole bridge.

"I so saw you about to hit that bar, but I thought it would be funny not to say anything. Hahaha," continued Mike.

I laughed and ignored him off. But fact of the matter remains is that he was no friend. If Mike hadn't had observed the hit and laughed then that would be fine.

Yawn! Forget that shit-head! The counts I can have on his ass they'd be no black in space.

That night carried on to then have Romeo start a fight with four white (British-English) guys at the bar, each twice the size of him minding their own business. Romeo had pushed them, they pushed back and I stepped in to apologize to them. What a moron my best friend Romeo, a day before the party where he is respected more from me respecting my own father, but he wanted me to walk into the party with a black eye. (Even on the day of the celebration I valued his friendship so great that I waited for him to come by my side before I thought to cut the cake).

On note, Romeo was a racist as far as I now have come to believe, racist to the white man and woman. He hated that I wore a Cross. He questioned my choice for Jesus. He got into the fight with those guys on that day. Once he punched a pillow after a white girl had got up from it and once he went to strike a white girl after a night out but she had miraculously had moved in another direction oblivious to the punch that came from Romeo. Ideally let's say Romeo wasn't a racist but was afraid that I would discover the truth and he would lose my need for him as an older male role model. Then again he did say he hated white people straight to my face. I never thought anything of this as how could I judge a race I never knew?

The Stage Hotel, party went well enough and everyone had a brilliant time at, 'SUNDEEP''s birthday. Oh, yes! Sundeep's 21st. Who was Sundeep? I knew a Sandeep. I asked my dad who made the banner, and he answered his youngest brother. I asked my uncle, who defended my dad and told me not to worry about it. I should have taken the banner down. To have taken the banner down gently, rolling it up to smoke it freely as I don't know no Sundeep! Millionaire Daddy couldn't spell his son's name. Oh My God!

"A person finds joy in giving an apt reply – and how good is a timely word!"   [Proverbs 15:23]

"To humans belong the plans of the heart, but from the Lord comes the proper answer of the tongue."
[Proverbs 16:7]

"Of what use is money in the hand of a fool, since he has no desire to get wisdom?"
[Proverbs 17:16]

"A good name is more desirable than great riches; to be esteemed is better than silver or gold."
[Proverbs 22:1]

"An honest answer is like a kiss on the lips."
[Proverbs 24:26]

After B.C.

What is very small, smaller that an adult finger tip, and is red with black spots with two white spots on their head? The red pigment is on an exoskeleton shell that can split into two to reveal wings under them. The creature can fly to say the least but rather uses their six legs to maneuver. The creature is harmless but one can become alarmed when unknowingly finds the creature on themselves. If one pokes at this creature that is small, the creature has two actions they can take. They can either become motionless hiding into their exoskeleton shell or can simply just fly away. Yes, they are ladybirds, or as the Americans would call them, ladybugs.

There were many ladybugs in my life in the first semester at Southern Wesleyan University. Sitting at the back of the class to the professor's left in his biology class on a wooden chair behind a wooden table; many ladybugs came to pay me attention. They would come from a crack beside the window frame behind me and find themselves on the table where I sat. I amused them as much as they were amusing me. I mostly allowed them to do as they pleased as I sat and listened to the professor for the hour whilst making notes.

Professor W.S. was aware that my attention was on the ladybugs, but as I was as quick as a fox and was repeating a class that I had taken many times in the past and passed, he allowed me to stay in trance with the ladybugs which I guess was pleasant for him also. What was one to say to a chap like me in the South, where the university had never had a British-Indian in their institute for a hundred years? Harmless nevertheless, they were ladybugs resting, playing, and maneuvering to and fro from the wooden table to the white paper of my notes to the shadows of my hovering hands.

"... go and make disciples of all nations, baptizing them in the name of the Father and of the Son and of the Holy Spirit, and teaching them to obey everything I have commanded you. And surely I am with you always to the very end of age."

[Matthew 28:19-20]

The boy at the gas station was around seven years old that had come in with his dad, a man with a proud appearance. There's nothing wrong with that as the man could have been Barak Obama. The man however wasn't Barak Obama, he was slightly darker than him. He came to the cash register to pay for his products. He had several products but just in that moment of time came a hand from behind him that held a twenty dollar note. Without considering the proud man's feelings

I took the note from the other man behind and registered into the second till for gasoline on pump one. (These multitasks I had done many of times).

"Pump one, good man," said the man from behind as the whole process was done in a blink of an eye saving him waiting for the man in front.

"What was that? I was here first," said the man who was first in a shocked tone.

"He who comes first, come last and he who comes last comes first," I replied in my British accent which made the man take a step back.

His boy looked up at me with amazement on realization on not how his proud father was valued, but how life had its way to better time itself. However what he said next I will never forget.

"Wow! I'll never forget this in my life."

"Dear children, let us not love with words or speech but with actions and in truth." [1John 3:18]

"I have no greater joy than to hear that my children are walking in the truth."   [3John 1:4]

Crows caw, caw, caw. Ravens caw, caw, caw. Roosters caw and peacocks coo. I have no idea why peacocks sound as that, but I have some idea why crows and ravens caw because of the critical thinking laid out by T.H. White in his famous book, 'The Once and Future King'. Crows caw as when they kill a mouse the mouse gives a squeak as a small caw, and there you have Merlin the Magician teaching Wart, young King Arthur of Camelot about how crows caw. White also mentioned in the same teaching why owls hoot and robins sing. As the wind that blows through the trees gives a, 'hoooot,' sound and as water whistles as it flows in streams, the owl and the robin that sit in trees and beside streams become accustomed to hoot and whistle respectively.

Crows, ravens and buzzards were very visible in the days of my rebirth. I heard that ravens signify rebirth, recovery, renewal, recycling, reflection and healing. Prophet Elijah was illustrated in many paintings feeding crows. I guess the significance allowed me to see the light out of the darkness from where I had come from.

Many people make stories of crows to be in a negative light, but if they would have lost as much as I did and gained nothing in return, no creature that shows peace is in a negative light. Poor crow or raven that has to live a life as such, nevertheless the Lord is the Maker of the bird, and He is also the Maker of the father that distracted this little boy from seeing the crows and ravens.

I've many stories of crows since my rebirth. I believe Lord Jesus Christ is watching over me when a crow flies by my vision unexpectedly. I turn my head and out of the horizon or over a building there is the beautiful creature with shiny black feathers just soaring in and out of sight.

In my anger there he is again, or she, or they. They are there in my anger providing me with reassurance and comfort. He flies by me as I drive looking to the right on an American road. He lands on branches as I exit my car. He appears over the crest of a building with a dozen more as I am to crush a wicked heart into the ground. There he is again just sitting on top of the gas station sign to give me company amongst thirty customers. There again lying on the floor dead as can be by either flying into a glass window or directly falling from the sky so high. Cover him with newspaper and put him on a plate, carry his flesh downstairs to rest his body on the earth below.

"Sing a song of sixpence,
A pocket full of rye,
Four and twenty blackbirds
Baked in a pie.
When the pie was opened
The birds began to sing —
Wasn't that a dainty dish
To set before the king?"

"Again Jesus said, "Peace be with you! As the Father has sent me, I am sending you." And with that he breathed on them and said, "Receive the Holy Spirit. If you forgive anyone's sins, their sins are forgiven; if you do not forgive them, they are not forgiven.""   [John 20:21-23]

Thank you very much, to the two spirits that stood at gas-pump five in the middle of the night during my graveyard shift for an hour or more. A man and a woman stood in the middle of an empty twelve gas-pump station talking to each other as it would appear to the next customer. The man who was an African-American who had arrived first to fill gasoline at gas-pump five and she who was also African-American who had come moments after parking her car at gas-pump six. They filled their cars with fuel by credit card at the pump and then just stood chatting for an hour or more as I did what I did inside the gas station.

Just a few moment before them had come a huge hefty African-American man from Washington D.C. which was approximately at one in the morning. As my doors were never locked when I was working he came in and in delight was amazed that the door opened to the building.

Now no harm intended as I was just making conversation as I did to everyone, but this man found offence to what I had said. When he first spoke and the fashion of his gait he came across as gay or 'camp' to me. So I asked him if he was. Immediately he became aggressive and defensive. He had turned red and in the coolness of the night had become hot under the collar. As many American's wanting to share their pride of their country to me, he emphasized he was from D.C. So I shouldn't mess with him. I stood watching him get his knickers into a twist marching around the store floor. He didn't buy anything but instead walked out and walked around even more in frustration and anger due to my simple spoken question. In all honesty I believe he was calming down from not attacking me, or thinking about attacking me, or being confronted outside his comfort zone just as lost as a candle lit at noon.

The spirits that had come moments after saw him walk out the building. They witnessed his behavior and stood to support me. The reason why they stood for so long was so to see what the man would do in his frantic state. They also witnessed me clean my property and do chores of business. They witnessed the excessively emotional man move his car from the bay beside the entrance to a parking spot facing the east horizon to the left of the building and fall asleep in his passenger seat.

I had nothing to worry about as a call to 911 was as easy as rolling up a stick of green herb and going outside to have the smoke. So I did just that. I rolled up a smooth smoke and in the early hours of the cool black night with a black bags in my hand went to have my smoke, change the bin liners of the trash cans, check on the sleepy head and cross my thanks to the spirits that saved us.

"But Abimelech said, "I don't know who has done this. You did not tell me, and I heard about it only today."
[Genesis 21:26]

Where there's a will, there's a way. The will was to smoke the magic herb, cannabis, ganja, whatever one wants or needs to call it, it's dope! Therefore I had met many people in the South that sold me the herb, but to me it wasn't about deal but about relations with the dealership.

I drove myself into the hood of Greenville. Yes, this was the hood and I was introduced to a very nice man with one eye. He name was, Sly. Sly with one good eye. Who knows if Sly was his birth name as for sure was not his Christian name, and for that what Sly called me as was, England. I assume the man in his late fifties, possibly in his seventies now knew my real name but out of respect for me or fear of me called me as that.

I got to know him really well. He wasn't a drug dealer; he was a momma's boy, looking after his mother too who was mostly in the next room. He lived in the hood all his life since the days his granddad and possibly dad were slaves. Sly surely was a slave in front of the red necks, however he had found the master of red necks, and so he was a double slave now and hence the name England.

Who knew if Sly sold more than marijuana, as surely he would not tell me. I was against all synthetic drugs now, that anyone in consumption of them would pay a hefty price in my finding. Plus Sly was a good man; he knew I had so much on my plate that a spot of weed was sanity.

He lived in a building that was two homes each having three rooms. (A lounge, a bedroom, a kitchen, oh and a small space for a shower and toilet). He lived, worked, slept in the lounge.

Early mornings before university, late evenings after working the second shift or before the graveyard shift, Sunday mornings, Saturday afternoons, Hospital visits, Thanksgiving, Christmas, Diwali, Independence Day, or just for the sake of days, even when he wasn't at home I was there. I chilled on his porch waiting for him or with him rolling one up and smoked.

I met the neighborhood too. Met everyone and everyone had nothing to say in depth to me besides, 'Jesus'. Where did I come from? Who was I that kept their pants pulled up? They knew that I worked at the gas station, and they knew that I went to the university in Central. But most of all they knew that as much as I liked to share and talk, I could also play deadly and silent. Respect from the cold winter days to the hot summer ones as the Honda with two front dents drove in and out of their Greenville neighborhood. Peace.

"There were as many men in Israel and Judah as the sand on the seashore, they ate, they drank, and they were happy." [1Kings 4:20]

'That's a heavy bike at gas-pump four,' I said to myself on yet another grave yard shift at Raceway. I admired the bike as the rider got off and filled gasoline into the tank. He was an American-English man in his late forties. There was no one else there. There was him, me, his bike, and the Lord. There was him, me, his bike, and the Lord moments after he finished filling up his tank still. But then there came something else. The man just stood by his bike for twenty minutes in a still like motion but occasionally shaking.

Minding my business minding my business, I thought nothing more until after another ten minutes still seeing the man standing by his bike at pump four shaking. Half an hour now had gone by and no other customers had come at two in the morning. Possibly someone did but this man was still there so I left my stand to go outside and see how he was doing or needing some assistance.

Cutting a long story shorter than this man's condition I will say he had Parkinson's Disease. I invited him into the building and asked him to rest. He was thankful as he just needed time for his medication to sink in. At times police would arrest him for the image they would see and by the time he could explain his condition he would be behind bars. He didn't have family, and he didn't have much money. He drove his bike up and down highways all across United States of America as that was his release from the dis-ease.

Once he got himself back to his frame of mind, we shook hands and he got onto his heavy bike and drove off south off Exit 40 onto the I-85 towards Miami.

"I have been crucified with Christ and I no longer live, but Christ lives in me. The life I now live in the body, I live by faith in the Son of God, who loved me and gave himself for me."

[Galatians 2:20]

Once upon a time in Easley, SC, there was a man named Rico. Rico was a cousin to Charles. Charles was my new found friend whilst working labour work after graduating from SWU. Charles was an African man that had just been released from jail for selling drugs. No, excuse me; he was a father to two children and husband to a wife that worked around the clock as he was in prison for selling drugs.

I spent many times and drives with Charles. He spoke quick and thought nothing more of me than what he got and that was curiosity. Anything that amused him from me he replied with a short chuckle, like 'hah'. That was his approval. (Whatever God, I love Jesus).

Charles had another cousin and his name was Antonio. No really his name was Antonio as far as I knew. He was a big black man at 6'4" built to the rim and out of jail too. No family besides the company he kept with the local youth. He lived by the railroad that ran by Easley.

Charles, Antonio and I were at Rico's. Oh by the way Rico was a hybrid man with a lovely lady and a lovely place, and for a living partly sold green herbs. Charles knew me best as of work, but they all kept edge of their transmission of neurotransmitters between their synapses of the neural and muscular system. Either that or as any black slave child in the business of selling me God's product were just waiting for me to slip, buckle, trip, taken for a fool, or to get the one up on someone that knew them better than the pictures of Christ they had in their homes.

One day to once upon a time came the awakening for Rico. More times than many I would meet with Rico for friendship and business without Charles or Antonio. Wherever I go I never come across as the nervous person or the shy as after all I lost a life due to that insecurity. So with Rico I would consider his place as mine. Not huge things like sleeping in his bed, but more switching on the television, getting myself a glass of water or using the toilet without asking permission. For me this is a man thing and other men would respect that a man doesn't need to ask for using the toilet.

But one afternoon out of paranoia, doubt, anxiety, nervousness, insecurity or whatever, Rico questioned our friendship and pulled a knife out the kitchen draw and to my face.

"What you playing at? Where did you come from and what the fuck are you doing here?! Who the fuck are you?! Get the fuck out of my house and take your shit with you!" he shouted whilst cutting my cheek slightly with the knife.

His wife at that moment ran down the stairs in her bathrobe with one of her breasts half hanging out to stop his behaviour. I opened the door and he practically pushed me out.

"Give me my merchandise I came for and my lighter! I will be at the gym and tomorrow I'll come back again after you've calmed down. If you want to see me before then you know where to find me!" I quickly replied back.

He threw my pack of smokes, herbs and lighter out and slammed closed the door. I went to the gym thinking about what had tripped him over.

The next day roughly the same time I knocked again on his door. No one gives me a bad name or thinks they can assume something about me which is not true, or make whatever story they like when I can set them straight I would save. Rico let me in and asked if I was okay. I said, 'I heal better than Jesus, so not to worry about it.' I sat at his high-stand kitchen table and he went to get 'something' for me to make.

"I don't know what came over you yesterday, but I guess I can imagine you're concerned about who I am in your house," I said. "I'll let you know you have nothing to worry about Rico. When I sit here I don't think about you, or anything that you can imagine. What I think about is, 'black'. You probably don't understand what I mean so I will tell you. You may need a glass of water after what I'm about to tell you."

He looked at me in bewilderment and curiosity about what I was about to say.

"When I'm here, I'm not looking at anything in particular but I'm seeing everything. You see I consider the colour, black, as peace and that's what I live by. 'Peace be upon you,' is what Christ Jesus said. And after all I have been through very late but better than never I have realised that black is a necessity in the light of God to respect. So I'm not looking at you or your wife or anything but that of the element of black. Under this placemat, the colour of that photo frame you have there, the frame of the television, your eyes, my eyebrows, the corner of this room, the horizon outside your window, this shadow under my hand," I said whilst moving my hand over the table.

Immediately Rico stood up, "follow me," he said and walked to the fireplace.

I followed and he switched on the fireplace. "Sit, make yourself at home. You want something to drink?" We smiled and shared a deep stare that still exists miles away to this very day.

Jesus Promises the Holy Spirit

""If you love me, keep my commands. And I will ask the Father, and he will give you another advocate to help you and be with you forever - the Spirit of Truth. The world cannot accept him, because it neither sees him nor knows him. But you know him, for he lives with you and will be in you. I will not leave you as orphans; I will come to you. Before long, the world will not see me anymore, but you will see me. Because I live, you also will live. On that day you will realize that I am in my Father, and you are in me, and I am in you. Whoever has my commands and keeps them is the one who loves me. The one who loves me will be loved by my Father, and I too will love them and show myself to them."

Then Judas (not Judas Iscariot) said, "But, Lord, why do you intend to show yourself to us and not to the world?"

Jesus replied, *"Anyone who loves me will obey my teaching. My Father will love them, and we will come to them and make our home with them. Anyone who does not love me will not obey my teaching. These words you hear are not my own; they belong to the Father who sent me.*

"All this I have spoken while still with you. But the Advocate, the Holy Spirit, whom the Father will send in my name, will teach you all things and will remind you of everything I have said to you. Peace I leave with you; my peace I give you. I do not give to you as the world gives. Do not let your hearts be troubled and do not be afraid.

"You heard me say, 'I am going away and I am coming back to you.' If you loved me, you would be glad that I am going to the Father, for the Father is greater than I. I have told you now before it happens, so that when it does happen you will believe. I will not say much more to you, for the prince of this world is coming. He has no hold over me, but he comes so that the world may learn that I love the Father and do exactly what my Father has commanded me.

"Come now; let us leave."

[John 14:15-31]

Glossary

Aalan wa shallan – Welcome, in Arabic.

Allah – The Creator, in Arabic.

Allah ka shokra – Thank God, in Arabic.

Almighty – A description fitting the Lord.

Amen – Lord let it be so, in Hebrew.

Amigo – Friend, in Spanish.

Apostles – Twelve brothers bound by the initial contact of the Gospel.

Arrepientanse, porque el reino de los cielos esta cerca. Mateo tres: cautro. – Repentant, as the kingdom of heaven is near. Matthew 3:4, in Spanish.

At arm's length – To be distant.

Balti – A Bangladeshi dish of vegetables or meat.

Benjamin – As in Benjamin Franklin.

Bhagavan – The Spirit of God, in Gujarati.

Bible – Holy Scripture of Christianity.

Black Stone – Ancient religious artifact in Mecca, Saudi Arabia, a.k.a. the Kabba.

Blunt – Marijuana rolled in cigar paper.

Brahman – A religious caste, in Hinduism.

Brown – As in Dr. Emmett Brown from 1985's trilogy; Back to the Future.

Brisket – meat from a cow's chest.

Buddha – abbreviation for Siddhartha Gautama.

Buddah –synonym for marijuana.

Budweiser – An American brewed beer.

Charotar Patidar Samaj – Group of people who are descendents of twelve ancient villages of overlapping farms in northwest India.

Compardre – Friend, in Spanish.

Consonant – Pleasing rhythm.

Corinthians – Letters wrote by Apostle Paul to the Corinthians around 55 to 90 A.D.

De Lorean – An American automobile.

Dios – God, in Spanish.

Dissonant – Tense rhythm.

Diwali – Hindu festival of lights. Day proceeds before the Hindu New Year Calendar.

Dichosos los Dios – Bless God, in Spanish.

Dukes of Hazzard – A Southern North American movie based around 1979.

En seguida que? – as what? in Spanish.

Espiritu Santo – Holy Spirit, in Spanish.

Eye – Millennium Eye, London, Westminster, UK.

Father – The Creator, in English.

FHM – For Him Magazine, magazine.

Folklore – Social customs from different cultures.

Ganga – synonym for marijuana.

God – The Creator, in English.

Gospel – To practice Christianity, also referred name for Jesus.

Gracis – Thank you, in Spanish.

Grand – synonym for a thousand in a currency.

Greenville Tech – Greenville Tech College, SC.

Hallelujah – Praise the Lord, in Hebrew.

Hansel & Gretel- Two characters from a German
  fairytale.

Harley – as in motor engine, Harley Davidson.

*Harmano –*Brother, in Spanish.

He – English Scripture for, The Creator.

High – sedated on cannabis.

Him – English Scripture for, The Creator.

Hiroshima – A Japanese city that was nuked
  bringing World War II to a close.

Holy Spirit – The Creator in spirit.

Hombre – Man, in Spanish.

Id – Acting on impulse for self-satisfaction.

Isaiah – A prophet describing sin to punishment
  from the time before Christ.

Jai Shree Krishna – Praise The Light, in Gujarati.

Jesucristo – Jesus Christ, in Spanish.

Jesus – The Creator in human form, the Messiah
  for the Jews and all mankind.

Joint – Marijuana and tobacco filled in rolling
  paper.

Kaka(s) – Father's brother(s), in Gujarati.

*Kama –*Feeling of relaxation, in Hindi.

Khalnayak – An outlaw, in Hindi.

Killing time – synonym for relaxing.

Kronenbourg – French Beer founded in 1664.

Kudha – God, in Urdu.

Kudha ki bhala, Aqbar ki dooha – God's grace and
  God's mercy, in Urdu.

La afham – I don't understand, in Arabic.

Lentamente y claramente – slowly and clearly, in Spanish.

Lord – The Creator, in English.

Mahabharatha – Indian Scripture based on an ancient war between kingdoms.

Mandir – Hindu Temple.

Marlboro – As in a packet of Marlboro branded cigarettes.

Masha'Allah – Beautiful Life / Beautiful God.

Mary-jane – synonym for marijuana.

Masa – Mother's sister's husband, in Gujarati.

Masi(es) – Mother's sister(s), in Gujarati.

Masoretes – Jewish scholars from 900 A.D. recording paths of suffering.

Masters of Evil – Comic villains from Marvel comics.

Merci – Thank you, in French.

Mount Golgotha – Hill where the Calvary for Jesus' crucifixion occurred in Jerusalem.

MRI – Magnetic Resonance Imaging, used to evaluate internal organ structure.

Nadine Gordimer – Poet from South Africa, 1923.

Naseeb – fate, in Urdu.

New Testament – Letters of the apostles gathered by Jewish scholars on the works of Jesus Christ. The second canon of the Holy Bible.

Newsagents –Confectionery Shop.

Nourta – Hindu festival.

Old Testament – Scripture written by Hebrew & Jewish scholars corresponding to the Tanakh & the Torah respectively. The first canon of the Holy Bible.

Om Shanti – Peace be with you, in Sanskrit.

Pagan – Someone who has not acknowledged those who have died for freedom and security.

Pea brain – having small knowledge.

Pea head – having a small brain.

Phantom heads – A manikin to practice dental operations on.

Play Station – Sony Entertainment System.

Pot – term for marijuana.

PTI – Pre-Trial Intervention.

Puff the magic dragon – phrase for marijuana.

Que sera sera – what will be will be, in Spanish.

Raj – Ruling between monarchies in India.

Ramayana – A story celebrating Diwali.

Samuel – Hebrew Prophet who made Saul and David kings of Israel.

Sanskrit – Ancient Indian Scripture.

Scripture – Writings of theology.

Shankar – synonym for Shiva, lord of evolution in Hindu Scripture.

Shivlinga – A stone that represents man and woman, a symbol of divine creation.

Shrink – synonym for psychologist.

Sikh – A community of people from Punjab (north-west India) who were approached by Prophet Guru Nanak to explain path to salvation.

Skunk – type of marijuana.

Spiderman – A comic hero from Marvel comics.

St. George – Saint of England.

Swami – Buddhist of Hindu theology.

S.W.U. – Southern Wesleyan University.

Taj Mahal – A beautiful ancient building in India made from marble.

THC - Delta-9-tetrahydrocannabinol.

The Creator – Theological Spirit living and knowing all from the heavens.

Timbre – Unique sounds instruments make.

Toda harmanas – All the sisters, in Spanish.

To-score – Find comfort from the opposite sex.

Universe – Everything inside the Heavens.

Vasoconstrict – Blood vessels contracting to increase the flow of blood around the body.

Walkers – Potato chip manufacturer, in Leicester.

DEEP TALES OF JESUS CHRIST

Tales of Jesus Christ, by Sandeep. (Xx = Jesus):

When Xx Met Paul:

One evening Xx, John, James, Peter and Andrew were walking by the Sea of Galilee, and were feeling hungry. They walked into the nearby tavern.

Peter walked to the bar man and asked, "What's on the menu?"

"Why don't you guys take a seat and I'll get the waitress to come serve you," said the bar man.

"I only want to know what's on the menu before we take a seat. So what's on the menu?" said again Peter.

"Why don't you guys take a seat and I'll get the menu for you?" returned the bar man.

"What's wrong with you man! We first want to see the menu," replied Peter.

"What's wrong with this man's hearing? We said we want to see the menu, mate." followed up Andrew.

"I said, I'll get you a menu if you kindly have a seat," continued the bar man.

"Listen Keeper, we would like to know what's on the menu first," added in John.

"Hey fool! Don't you know who we are with? Now just give us a menu so we can decide to stay or to leave before we sit!" interrupted James.

"Who you calling fool?! I don't care if you're with King David. If you want to eat then just take a seat!" directly declared bar man.

Peter forwarded, "Cheeky man. Can't even deliver a simple request."

Peter rolled his eyes and tried to make his own way to the tavern kitchen.

Outraged the bar man shouted, "where are you going?!"

He then blocked Peter's path, grabbed him and pushed him away from the kitchen door. Peter fell onto the floor. Seeing this Andrew tried to punch the man, but he was blocked and thrown onto his brother. Then James stepped in, but quick as a flash the man put his head into a bowl of mash potatoes. So John dove thereafter, however was hit so hard that he fell onto a table dropping gravy, meat and ale onto the floor. James and Peter got up to attack the man again, however Xx moved in and pick up John to sit him on a chair, and whilst moving James and Peter out the way from the man he stood Andrew back onto his feet. Nevertheless in all this commotion the man launched into Xx and held him with both hands against the wall. Suddenly the man fell into shock as he felt supreme energy radiating like the light of the Lord coming from Xx.

"Holy God! What are you?" asked the man.

With a smile Xx replied, "I am He."

The man let go of Xx, and a cry came from the kitchen, "Paul! Paul! Are you fighting again?"

Paul replied, "no momma!"

"We'll have five plates though," Xx added.

Grace given, food eaten, fellowships begun.

When Xx Met John and James:

One peaceful night with a full moon reflecting off Sea of Galilee, two brothers were preparing their fishing nets for the following day on their boat at the end of a pier when from a fair distance a sweet voice cried out, "John and James, brothers of thunder, come follow me!"

James and John looked towards the direction of the voice and saw a tall slender figure with long wavy hair as a silhouette from the moonlight.

"Come here to us!" shouted back John.

"I wonder why she wants us to follow her? Maybe she's hungry for some action," James said.

As the person walked slowly down the pier to the boat the moonlight rose from their feet to their head by the time they climbed onto the boat.

"DAAAAM!" hollered both brothers. You are not a woman, but a handsome man! O Lord!"

"Sorry, forgive me, I have a cold. My name is Xx, and from this day forth you will catch men as well as fish for the one who has sent me."

He laughed. Xx explained. They laughed.

When The Guards Came:

Within a building the apostles of Christ listened to the last words of Father given to Xx overnight and into the early hours of a new day there came a heavy knock at the door.

"Who is it?" asked Thomas.

"It's the guards of Pharisee, open up!"

"What do you want?"

Without a reply the door was forced opened.

"Xx come forward!" one of them ordered.

"The Pharisee orders your crucifixion."

"We do not know any Xx," said Peter.

"You lie, your accent gives you away. Now bring him forward or we'll have you all arrested!"

"I am Xx," said John stepping forward.

"I am Xx," said Andrew stepping forward.

"I am he you seek," James proclaimed.

"The man you search is I," said Philip.

"No, I am the one," said Bartholomew.

Matthew stepped forward, "I am Xx,"

"No, I am the one you seek," Judas added.

"Haha, I am Xx," said the other James

"Xx is I," said Simon the Zealot.

"Fool, I am him," declared Thaddaeus.

"Enough! Take them all!" said the guard.

Xx kicked over a jug of water which flowed to the apostles' feet. Xx then answered, "I am the face you are afraid to see. I am the son of Joseph, the son of Mary. I am the right hand of Almighty Father. I am the Son of God."

Baptism of Xx:

All people of Nazareth were at the riverbank of the River Jordan waiting in turn for John the Baptist, to baptise them in the water. As was written Xx had come to John the Baptist and asked John to baptise him. However John the Baptist said that Xx should baptise him as that would be proper. So first John the Baptist placed Xx under the water close to fear and raised him out. Then the sky opened and a voice from Heaven called to Xx declaring him as God's son. The Spirit of God in the form of a turtle dove came from the open sky and gave Xx the power of the Holy Spirit and Fire, in the form of peace and love. The people who witnessed this were amazed and afraid.

"My turn! My turn, O holy one!" said John.

So Xx held John under water. He was still in thought of what God had said and felt the Lord's spirit around him. Xx looked around to see if the dove was to be seen. He saw the dove fly over him and to a nearby tree branch. There were bubbles and splattering coming from John, but Xx was in awe of his Father and carried on the baptism. A little too late Xx released John's head from under the water but John didn't come out refreshed.

"The spooky man has murdered over baptism's with John! We are done for! There's no one to save us from our sins!" shouted a person.

"Get that man who has damned us!" shouted out another person.

Xx was shocked the people had become a mob. Before Xx could think about John the Baptist he began making his way out of the river. He left his sandals by the riverbank and ran as fast as he could home. He made his way to the top of a hill where the mob was too weak to climb and hid.

"Thank you Xx," said John's ghost. "You have no idea how annoying the people were getting. They are all yours now. I am relieved."

"Don't worry, I gotcha back," said the Lord.

Xx felt a shiver and sneezed one out aloud.

Correlation of the Gospels to the Gospel

Setting the scene I worked as a community support worker for a period of my life. One of my clients with learning disabilities wore a cross around his neck and claimed that the cross was his God. He also had the same name as one of the four gospels of Jesus Christ. (The first four letters in the NTTT). So I explained to him in a way he could understand how the brethren's stories linked to the life of Lord Jesus Christ, and thus the importance of his name.

Matthew (Merchant): Jesus, the son of David, who was the Son of God. He walked down the seashore pass the fishermen to get to The Shop. Once he was at The Shop, the man named Jesus bought him a lollipop and enjoyed what God had given him.

Mark (Labourer): There was a dude. The dude's name was Jesus and he was a cool dude. He was one voice in the wilderness. Dude went to the shop pass the sea and dying for a lollipop, Jesus got himself a one. He tasted by licked it and enjoyed it.

Luke (Physician): There was once a great man who lived in Nazareth, and his name was Jesus Christ. Son of Joseph, but really the Son of God as a descendent of King David. Yes Jesus, the King of Jews, had a sweet tooth and by the Sea of Galilee where he was baptised he walked to the convenience store known as The Shop, and here he asked the store keeper for their finest lollipop. Jesus bought the lollipop and radiating his smile he devoured the lollipop with every sense of his taste. This satisfied his sugar intake and his day to come.

John (Fisherman): O Mighty God had placed His son with a taste of sugar. The nectar of God was placed in Jesus. So Jesus Christ, (the living God) walked pass the great sea where God had spoken and brought the Holy Spirit to him to get to The Shop. The Son of the Almighty went to The Shop by the sea to get himself a sugar treat. Jesus by the water and The Shop prayed and got him a lollipop. The lollipop was as godly as the daylight. The day cooled as Christ Jesus, the brother of us Gospels licked and enjoyed the flavour. As God loved His son, he too loved us and the lollipop.

About the Author

My name is Sandeep Patel. I had thought of writing stories since I was young. In those days I read stories about action heroes from Marvel and D.C. comics. In those days I did not appreciate much for the artists or the fact that Superman was created by Jerry Siegel and Joe Shuster. What fascinated me the most was the stories they told.

Shankar was my old self before I was brought to consciousness. Being in the appraisal of Shankar had helped me write this novel. School recited in a manner which followed an interest in science and religion, all things that worked and all things that moved.

The approach to the way that Shankar relaxed and studied appealed to me, he was dangerous as well as approachable on agreement to only fear the Lord. Now I have the strength to hold Shankar but I wish I could have sooner. If I lived in ancient times I would believe whole heartedly in ancient ways, but I live in the time of global communication and what makes sense is if we all begin to live through the apostles' love for their brother, the Son of God.

I read literature from different centuries as a scholar would to understand great aspirations and their adaptations for human survival. From reading about different cultures I began to get a better understanding of my own. I am of Gujarati descent meaning my first language comes from India. The heritage follows and so do customs and traditions. This brought me to understand that man is far different from animal. For instance man can take care of animal but animal cannot hospitalize man. My critical thinking became alive and my interest to learn wherever grew exponentially.

I am twenty-nine (2009) and still curious about what made Thomas Edison tick. My faith reaches one who is far greater in our hearts than all of space, like Jesus I can love forever. My goal is to teach and minister the Word of God and bring joy. I hope to carry Shankar's strength and teach young ones wisdom as well as knowledge so they can prosper and die old, die well and give well to their life.

Spending time as Jesus Christ has come as a gift. I'm now much more grounded in belief that Jesus is well saturated within me. I believe in the nonphysical and that love is the only way to reach the Lord. Lord Jesus Christ can hold the love much greater than human, which is his burden. I was not good at handling answers before I praised a Father who could hear my questions. I, like my ego of Shankar speak only about my likes and dislikes, emphasising on likes, like what to eat, or where that best taste would be.

I enjoy living alongside Jesus' emotions. The emotion to desire a brighter, secure future.

Three egos fit this emotion of mine the best; One of that from The Light, One of that of loving Jesus Christ, and One of that of Shankar loving the people. This comforts me from every blow that I have endorsed, plus prevents me from intense suffering in the future. I am not a violent man; I am a good man, a good man! I've learnt how to keep patience and not to be afraid of calling a police over the paramedic if needed. The work Jesus Christ has shown me is not one to be excused as now my thought, power and love only climbs, all I have to decide is how fast? I believe that our youth should walk in the truth of the Lord, and as a reward we are rewarded with peace.

I enjoy all the beauty in life that is associated between the sky and the sand, and the sand with the sea. I would like to thank my schools for making my path straight and bridge constructors for their occupation. There's plenty of work to be done, recycling, inspiring and thickening the glory of love for God. This is what I believe we should live and fight for.

I wish to write more and create only the fear of the Lord. Nothing more but for all man-kind whenever, wherever they are to reach further out to the stars and maintain the growth of love, laughter and their will to live for one another forevermore.

Once upon a time a man parked his car perpendicular to the parking bays as to be able to see how his pumps at his gas station were doing and also bring a sense of excitement to young boys and girls. One late cold night a police car came and parked up alongside in a bay and then came another and parked alongside in a bay either side of the man's parked car. Both police officers came into the gas station where the man was working and got themselves snacks and drinks. Whilst they did this the man ran out from behind the registers (cashier tills), into the cold night outside and took a photo of his car parallel to his building perpendicular to the other two and walked back to the register. They exchanged small talk and processed the transaction of goods. The policemen got back into their vehicles and went back into the night leaving the man. They then all lived happily ever after. Amen.

Other Books by Author

Bhagavan's Guitar
As Light Is

A Potion
Light

Colours of Enlightenment
Right On Time

Colours of Enlightenment
and A Potion

Dear Terry

thanks for...

26/7/22.

Printed in Poland
by Amazon Fulfillment
Poland Sp. z o.o., Wrocław

91098568R00132